Start Mushrooming

2ND Edition

The Reliable Way to Forage

Stan Tekiela

Adventure Publications
Cambridge, Minnesota

Dedication

To my father, who first inspired me to hunt wild mushrooms.

Cover and book design by Lora Westberg

Edited by Sandy Livoti

Photo credits by photographer and page number:
Cover photos: front cover by beats1/Shutterstock.com; back cover by Mikhail Abramov/Shutterstock.com

Keith A. Bradley: 91(Berkeley's polypore); **Teresa Marrone:** 16 (pores), 24 (volva inset), 46 (bottom inset), 47, 53 (lower left), 60 (bottom); **Andrew Parker:** 54 (fibrous single stem), 59 (*Laetiporus confericola*); **Ron Spinosa:** 45 (gabled false morel); **Stan Tekiela:** 9, 10-11, 16 (top and bottom), 18 (top), 24 (amanita annulus), 25, 29, 34 (left and middle), 36 (gills), 38 (oyster and giant puffball), 39 (hen-of-the-woods and chanterelle), 40, 43, 46, 48 (whole morel), 58, 64, 66-67, 68, 69, 70 (gills), 82, 88, 93, 128; **kathryn.weiss:** 24 (white spores inset), 27; **Kathy Yerich:** 90, 95

Used under license from Shutterstock.com:
3d-sparrow: 100, 102, 104, 106, 107, 108, 110 (baskets); **AleksandarMilutinovic:** 12; **Alexander62:** 30-31; **Alexey Borodin:** 96-97; **Ananaline:** 41, 49, 57, 65, 73, 89 (season icons); **AntoinetteW:** 77; **Bildagentur Zoonar GmbH:** 24 (white gills inset), 83; **bogdan ionescu:** 52; **Brent Hofacker:** 114-115; **DnG Photography:** 78 (lower right); **Eileen Kumpf:** 50; **el_cigarrito:** 26 (left); **EM Arts:** 86 (right); **Epine:** 98-101 (recipe border, top); **gstalker:** 38 (shaggy mane); **Guenter Albers:** 98-99 (background); **HandmadePictures:** 118; **Hemerocallis:** 45 (false morel); **iremt:** 42; **JerHetrick:** 62; **JIANG HONGYAN:** 116; **Jiang Zhongyan:** 33, 44; **Kaiskynet Studio:** 36 (left), 70 (left); **Krungchingpixs:** 6-7; **Laurentiu Nica:** 24-29, 45, 61, 85 (skull and crossbones); **margouillat photo:** 99 (morel); **Matauw:** 112-113; **Mateusz Sciborski:** 72; **Mikhail Abramov:** 15 (top); **Mircea Costina:** 4-5; **Monticola:** 80; **mr.kie:** 78 (left); **nadtochiy:** 39 (sulfur shelf), 122-123; **Nikolay Kurzenko:** 91 (inset); **NinaM:** 39 (morel); **Olpo:** 94; **Pi-Lens:** 120; **Pixeljoy:** 15 (bottom); **PRILL:** 17; **Przemyslaw Muszynsk:** 54 (center); **Randy R:** 53 (upper right); **rng:** 21; **Roland Magnusson:** 86 (left); **sheris9:** 51; **SSSHY:** 56; **Tim Masters:** 117; **Timmary:** 119; **Tomasz Czadowski:** 18-19; **TYNZA:** 46 (top inset); **vector illustration:** 28, 52, 53, 59, 60, 74, 83, 91 (caution symbol); **Viktoriya Podgornaya:** 13; **Vlad Siaber:** 24 (death cap); **Vlasto Opatovsky:** 23; **Volodymyr Nikitenko:** 33

The following Mushroom Observer (mushroomobserver.org) images are used in this book. Individual photographers are listed in the credits above:
111776, 209748, 323007, 552866, 642899, 659207, 669070, 826316, 858833

The Mushroom Observer images below are licensed under the Attribution-ShareAlike 3.0 Unported (CC BY-SA 3.0) license, which is available here: https://creativecommons.org/licenses/by-sa/3.0/
Ann F. Berger: 61 (669070); **Joshua C. Doty:** 60, upper left (552866); **Patrick Harvey:** 34 and 45, big red false morel (323007); **Kady Hoffman:** 74 (826316); **Mike369:** 85 (659207); **Steve Ness:** 59, lower left (642899); **Ron Pastorino:** 26, right (858833); **Tim Sage:** 54, left inset (209748); **Robert Zuberbuhler:** 75 (111776)

10 9 8 7 6 5

Start Mushrooming: The Reliable Way to Forage
First Edition 1993
Second Edition 2019
Copyright © 1993 and 2019 by Stan Tekiela
Published by Adventure Publications
An imprint of AdventureKEEN
310 Garfield Street South
Cambridge, Minnesota 55008
(800) 678-7006
www.adventurepublications.net
ISBN 978-1-59193-830-9 (pbk.); ISBN 978-1-59393-831-6 (ebook)

Start

Mushrooming

2ND Edition

The Reliable Way to Forage

Morel

Morel Quest

The madness overtakes you,
It creeps into your mind.

It's an all-consuming feeling,
A quest that happens all the time.

The quest begins in spring or summer,
Depending on where you live.

Search under last year's foliage,
Your fingers as the sieve.

Look beneath the passing elms
Right after the life-giving rains.

Search high in the apple orchards,
Search low on riverbanks

For the elusive morel,
And then give thanks—

Thanks to our loving earth.

Table of Contents

Oyster

Enjoying the Wild Mushrooms

Have you ever walked through a wooded area with mushrooms growing and reminisced about your grandparents gathering some for the table? Did you wonder how they got their knowledge of mushrooms? In just a few short decades, we seem to have lost the information that people passed down from generation to generation. With this book, I hope to reconnect you with the tradition of mushroom hunting and help you experience a fascinating part of the natural world. Once you delight in the discovery of a patch of morels or prepare a dish of oyster mushrooms for your family, you'll want to keep that tradition going!

Over 25 years ago, as a new author and mushroom enthusiast, I wrote *Start Mushrooming* to introduce novices to six common, edible mushrooms. Today, I am happy to report that I still search the fields and woods for these tasty treats! In this new second edition, I added a seventh edible mushroom, the chanterelle, as a bonus. This orange beauty is not only highly sought for its delicate flavor, but it also often pops up in enough abundance to make it a meal.

Other current mushroom books often list scores of species, with hundreds of pages of illustrations, photos and descriptions to study for identification. This updated edition of *Start Mushrooming* remains a unique and much more practical guide. Here, before you start hunting, you'll learn about a select group of seven easy-to-identify, edible mushrooms. These mushrooms have several distinct characteristics, and with careful study, they are unlikely to be confused with others.

Start Mushrooming helps keep your hunt easy and focused in simple and straightforward ways. The easy check-off guide, along with the photos, will help guide you on your hunt.

Mushroom hunting is a great way to get into the field, enjoy some fresh air and get some exercise—but it's not just for those good things alone. I still firmly believe that the more we experience the outdoors and feel our connection to the natural world, the more we'll make better choices to care for it. My fascination for all things wild still burns bright, and I hope you will find the same is true for you in the wonderful world of mushrooms.

Enjoy the Wild Mushrooms!

Oyster

Get Ready to Hunt!

For several days now, you have felt the pull of the woods.

Last week's rain and warm temperatures have set the stage.

Your hiking stick and basket wait patiently by the door.

It is almost time to go.

The years of hunting mushrooms with your father have paid off.

It's mushroom hunting season again, and you wouldn't miss it for the world!

Oyster

BEFORE YOU BEGIN

How to Identify Mushrooms

This book has two reliable features for mushroom identification. It focuses on seven edible mushrooms that are easy for a novice to identify, and it provides a check-off guide for each mushroom to help you learn to identify your find.

In each check-off guide, six characteristics are given regarding the mushroom's season, habitat, appearance, cap, gills and stem. Use the check-off guide, together with the photos, to help you confirm that your mushroom is one of the seven.

Shaggy mane

While it may be tempting to go right to the check-off guide and head for the woods, it's very important that you don't. Accurate background information is necessary and can be gained by using the book as it is laid out. You'll need this background to use the check-off guide.

Learn what a mushroom is, how it develops and the terminology for its parts.

Learn when, where and how to hunt. Learn the basics of collecting.

Before you leave the house, learn about poisonous mushrooms. The best defense is a good offense.

Become familiar with the check-off guide and how it works.

Read about each of the selected seven edible mushrooms. Study the text, the check-off guide and the photos. In subsequent seasons, after you have some experience with using all of the information provided, you may only need to refer to the seasonal quick-guide that follows the text.

Do all of the reading first. Then focus your hunt and bring this book with you. Once you've found your treasure, compare your specimens to the text and photos, and be sure to compare with photos in other books. Then go through the check-off guide. If you can assuredly answer "yes" to each of the six characteristics, it's likely you have the right mushroom. But it's your responsibility to confirm your find. If you're not certain that you've found the correct mushroom, don't eat it.

Harvest according to the rules suggested. Bring home the bounty and use the delicious recipes to enhance and embellish the experience. At this point, I'll guarantee that you've discovered a new passion!

General Cautions

There are many edible wild mushrooms other than the seven featured in this book. Until you're certain that you can identify your finds (and differentiate them from the toxic and inedible species that may grow side by side), don't collect any mushrooms other than the safe seven recommended here.

To add to your knowledge, considering taking an accredited course on mushrooming or gathering with a professional mushroom expert or mycologist. Be aware,

Morel

however, that mushroom identification is sometimes difficult even for experts, so always use caution when collecting for the table.

When collecting mushrooms in the fall, be familiar with local deer and small game hunting seasons, and avoid hunting zones or wear bright orange clothing. When collecting on private property, always obtain the owner's permission. It may help to offer some of the bounty for their kindness.

State and national parks don't allow the collection of plants, but many will allow mushroom collection. Check with the park rangers or manager to get permission. Remember, you represent mushroom hunters across the country, so use good judgment when on public and private lands. You'll be surprised just how many people are interested in wild mushrooms; be ready to answer questions.

If you go mushroom hunting alone, tell someone where you will be and when you may be expected to return. Learn to recognize and stay away from poisonous plants, such as stinging nettles, poison ivy/oak and wild parsnip. If you come in contact with one of these, be sure you know how to best treat the rash, or consult your doctor. Wear long pants to protect against insects and a hat for sun protection. A walking stick is helpful in many situations and can be fashioned from nearly any stick.

Now, you're ready to learn how to start mushrooming!

My father placed his hand on my shoulder to suggest we should slow down. In a soft voice I could hear him say, "This is the place. Keep a sharp eye."

Our dog ran ahead wildly. She had no interest in wild mushrooms. It was the scent of the woods that guided her.

Even though many years have passed, I can still hear my father's voice echo in the forest breeze, always present and guiding as if he were still by my side.

And as long as I forage these woods, I know he always will be there.

Chanterelle

MUSHROOM LINGO

What Is a Mushroom?

So what is a mushroom? This question is easy to answer in technical terms, but the trick is to translate the scientific terms into commonly accepted words.

First, mushrooms are not members of the plant kingdom. They don't function like plants or have similar structures, and referring to them as plants is technically wrong. Don't fall into this trap.

Second, I have used the word "mushroom" throughout this book when I am actually talking about fungus. "Mushroom" is the most common and widely accepted term that refers to the fruiting body of a fungus. It may help to think of picking a mushroom as you would pick an apple from a tree: both are a reproductive structure. Unlike a tree, the vegetative part of the fungus that produces the mushroom is generally not visible because it grows as tiny threads within the soil or wood. That's why mushrooms have had such a mysterious past. People thought they just popped up overnight and didn't understand that the vegetative part of the mushroom had been growing there all along.

The Cap

The cap is generally the top of the mushroom and comes in many sizes, shapes and colors. The technical word for the cap is "pileus" and refers to a hat or cap worn by ancient Romans. You may immediately think of the dome-shaped cap that you've seen on typical store-bought mushrooms, but several of the safe seven mushrooms don't have a clearly defined cap.

Cap

The cap can be flat and semicircular, as seen in the oyster mushroom, or cone-shaped or oval with many pits and ridges, as seen in the morel. In any case, the cap is the uppermost portion of the mushroom and is immediately above the gills or pores.

Gills

The Gills

Although not all mushrooms have gills, in gilled species, the gills are found under the cap. Gills are thin, flat, blade-like radiating structures, much like pages in a book. On the surface of the gills, microscopic spores are produced and released for reproduction. Spores are the mushroom's version of seeds. By a variety of methods, the gills release tens of millions of microscopic spores into the air.

Pores

The Pores

Some mushrooms have tiny holes, called pores, in place of gills that serve the same purpose. Some mushrooms, such as the puffball, don't have obvious gills or pores but produce their spores within the mushroom. Distinguishing between these types is easy because the checkoff guide details their presence or absence and the choice will be obvious.

Stem

The Stem

The stem or stalk is technically called a stipe. Although it doesn't carry nutrients like the stem of a green plant, it shares the same common name. Stems can be thick or thin, brittle or fibrous, and attach to the cap in a variety of ways. A common attachment point is at the center of the cap, but stems can also attach at the side or edge. Many mushrooms don't have a stem because the caps are attached directly to the growing surface.

Regardless of the attachment, stems have one function: to get the cap up into the air to release the spores.

The Spores

As a mushroom matures, it casts off tens of millions of spores to be carried away on the wind. If a spore lands in a suitable place, it will produce small thread-like structures, called hyphae. These will grow into a thread-like network, called a mycelium, which is the vegetative portion of the fungus where the mushroom will be produced. Then the cycle begins again, assuring that there will be more mushrooms for the next generation of hunters to start mushrooming.

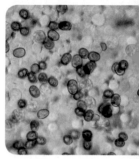

Spores

MUSHROOM HUNTING STRATEGIES

How to Focus Your Search

Knowing how to identify mushrooms is only part of the battle. The most successful mushroom hunters understand what a mushroom is and how it grows. You wouldn't search for morel mushrooms on the stumps of dead trees in autumn if you had knowledge of morels. Knowing the characteristics of mushrooms, such as the growing season and the habitat, are critical to finding them. These characteristics are incorporated into the text and the check-off guide for each mushroom.

The small group of mushroom hunters had been searching Mystic Valley for three days without success. The spirits of the hunters had plummeted. If only they could locate their mushroom treasure!

Two days passed before they discovered any trace. A faint, pleasant aroma radiated from all around. Knowing that air currents travel from low to high elevations, the group began their descent with a renewed enthusiasm.

"This must be the spot, the smell is so strong," someone said. As the group spread out, some fell to their knees for a better vantage point.

A cry rang out. "I've found them!"

Let's start with the season. Mushrooms are seasonal, so you need to know when they occur. If the mushroom you wish to gather appears in the fall, then it makes no sense to look for it on a spring walk. Of course, if you happen to come across a good habitat for spring mushrooms, make a mental note to return in the spring. Some mushrooms can occur in more than one season.

While the season for any particular mushroom is consistent, the exact timing for the appearance varies from year to year, just as weather varies within a season. You might happen upon a mushroom while on a bike ride or a walk. This is a sure sign that the conditions are right and it's time to get serious about the hunt.

Typical mushrooms are about 90 percent water, so moisture is very important to their existence. Most mushrooms occur in the spring and fall because that's when growing conditions (humidity, temperature) are best. The amount of moisture available prior to a season directly affects the timing of when mushrooms appear. Depending on the rainfall and temperature, some years are better for mushroom growth than others.

You'll want to hit the woods during a wet summer. Searching during or after an extended warm and rainy period is usually productive. Not only will you come up with more mushrooms, but you'll also enjoy the deep, rich appearance of the woods at these times. Since most

Morel season lasts four to five weeks

people stay indoors when it's wet, you'll have little competition and will enjoy the solitude.

If you haven't hunted a particular mushroom before, it will be helpful to spend some time studying the photos in this book to develop a mental image of the mushroom, especially when hunting for morels, which are masters at hiding. Fix the color, shape, size and texture into a mental image so that your mind is more open to seeing the mushrooms you are collecting. Bring this book and refer to the photos and the check-off guides frequently.

When hunting for mushrooms that grow on the ground, it is important to get down close to them. This reduces the angle of sight and allows more of the mushroom to be seen. On family hikes, children can help search for mushrooms. They are closer to the ground and have an advantage over adults when it comes to spotting these elusive treasures. Find a likely habitat, and then have them crouch down and scan the ground ahead of them.

Some mushrooms are well camouflaged and can be easily missed by untrained eyes. A walking stick can gently move the vegetation in order to find hidden mushrooms. This technique is essential in finding morel mushrooms.

Most mushrooms in this book tend to be large and obvious and require only a slow walk in the woods to be discovered.

When looking for larger mushrooms that grow on trees or on the ground, I have found that visual scanning works best. Simply look from side to side, scanning the area in a sweeping motion, without fixing your sight on any specific object. Look for shapes and colors that are inconsistent with the rest of the woods. This technique also works well for spotting birds and other wildlife. A good pair of binoculars will help to determine if something in the distance is a mushroom or just part of an irregular tree branch.

Their neighbor, basket in hand, was stooped over the soldierlike mushroom.

As they watched her fill the basket, concern and apprehension grew on their faces. With wrinkled brows they asked the inevitable, "You're not going to eat those, are you?"

"But, of course, I am," she grinned. "Meet me back at the cabin in a half hour."

It wasn't long before they succumbed to the aroma of Grandma's shaggy mane recipe and ate their words for dessert.

It is not important to have a large wooded area to hunt; mushrooms know no boundaries and will grow in urban and suburban settings. As long as there is a source of nutrients and moisture, the mushrooms will grow. Avoid lawns, roadsides, golf courses and areas that have been treated with herbicides and pesticides. Mushrooms absorb these chemicals, and you would be ingesting them directly. As hunters of wild mushrooms, we are again personally confronted with the contamination of our environment. However, this should spur us to become a stronger voice for a healthier planet.

An important factor in the success of a mushroom hunter is luck. Knowing when and how to look for mushrooms is essential, but a certain degree of luck helps.

Over time, you'll discover places that will become your favorite hunting grounds. Even though mushrooms seem to pop up overnight, the unseen portion of the fungus has been growing for many years and will continue to grow there year after year until the nutrients have been exhausted. Return to your hunting grounds each new season to harvest these delightful treats. I have many secret hunting spots that I return to every year. Like old friends, the mushrooms are patiently waiting for us to harvest them.

In many areas of the country, the location of favorite hunting grounds is a well-guarded secret that hunters would rather take to the grave than tell. If a mushroom hunter does tell you where to look for mushrooms, it might be to sidetrack you from the mother lode or to send you on a wild-goose chase. In either case, the secret of the seasoned mushroom hunter is protected. Remember, when you start mushrooming, harvest selectively and with respect.

PLAN AHEAD FOR THE HARVEST

Recommendations for the Field

The tools for collecting mushrooms are not expensive or difficult to obtain. Use a wicker basket with a handle or strap, or for large mushrooms, a wicker backpack. Plastic buckets are functional, but wicker baskets protect the mushrooms while allowing good air circulation, which keeps the specimens fresh. Don't use plastic bags for collecting; by the time you get the mushrooms home they will have started to decompose. A paper bag will serve well until you find an appropriate basket.

Oyster

Use a knife to carefully cut the mushrooms at the base to avoid disturbing the mycelium. A medium-sized lock-blade knife is the safest to use. Don't take all of the mushrooms from one area. Leave some behind so they can continue to cast off spores that will bring forth future mushrooms. It may be difficult to leave some behind, but this is an environmentally ethical thing to do.

Leaving some mushrooms behind is also beneficial for wildlife. Deer, squirrels and some insects, for example, depend on mushrooms as a food source. Squirrels will often gnaw off a mushroom and carry it up a tree to a branch, wedging it between twigs to dry. Look for tree branches decorated with drying mushrooms left by squirrels preparing for winter.

Upon finishing dinner, the entire family sat down to let the fare settle in, while the family cat helped herself to the leftover wild mushrooms.

"Shoo, down from there," came the instruction from the other room. "She sure likes those wild mushrooms!"

Forty-five minutes passed before the writhing and meowing began. They had never seen their beloved pet in such ill condition.

"If the cat is sick, then maybe it's only a matter of time for us."

Within the hour the family was explaining the story to the emergency room doctor. Stomach pumps were ordered, and at midnight the ill-fated family finally returned home.

"Someone should check on the cat."

Upon inspection, the group discovered six new additions to the family. Their cat had been in labor, and not sick at all.

Always cook all wild mushrooms before eating them! The cell walls of all mushrooms contain chitin (pronounced "KITE-n"). Chitin can swell in the stomach and cause pain if it is not cooked first. It is important to understand that chitin is not a toxin, but rather a substance that is difficult to digest. To avoid excess chitin, collect only the fresh, tender parts of any wild mushroom, and cook thoroughly. The same can be said for indulging in too many mushrooms at one time. As with any new food, eat wild mushrooms in moderation.

When you first start mushrooming, eat only one mushroom species at a time. While the safe seven mushrooms are not poisonous, some people may have certain sensitivities to them. In the rare event that you have a reaction to one mushroom species but not another, you'll know which species to avoid in the future. Collect only fresh mushrooms, just as you would select only fresh produce in the store. Avoid any mushrooms that are swollen, bruised, wet, spongy, limp or obviously past their prime.

Do not put unidentified mushrooms in the same basket that contains the edible mushrooms. Small pieces of unknown mushrooms can get mixed in with the edibles. Collect the unknowns at another time or use a different basket. Before harvesting any mushroom, read and review *Confronting the Enemy* on pp. 24–29.

When hunting and harvesting, take this book with you. You'll want to compare the mushrooms with the photos and text provided. Go through the check-off guide carefully to document that each of the distinguishing characteristics is present.

Giant puffball

CONFRONTING THE ENEMY
What about Poisonous Mushrooms?

The best way to protect yourself from an enemy in any situation is to know all about it—what it is and what it looks like. That's your best strategy as a mushroomer, too.

Begin learning the poisonous mushrooms a few at a time, just like the edible mushrooms. Poisonous mushrooms come in many colors, shapes and sizes, but the most obvious group of poisonous mushrooms is the genus *Amanita*. This genus includes some of the most deadly species. They are abundant and among the easiest mushrooms to identify as a group.

Death cap

Four Features of Poisonous Amanita Mushrooms

FEATURE	DESCRIPTION	SPECIES
Volva	A cup-like structure at the base of the stem.	Tawny grisette *Amanita fulva*
Annulus	A skirt-like ring around the stem.	Fly agaric *Amanita muscaria*
White gills	Thin, flat and blade-like structures under the cap.	Fly agaric *Amanita muscaria*
White spores	A spore print shows white spores.	*Amanita*

Learn to recognize the four characteristics of poisonous *Amanita* mushrooms. While these features are not always obvious, looking for these mushroom characteristics will help you identify a poisonous mushroom. A poisonous Amanita mushroom is indicated when all four of these features are present.

Even the deadliest of mushrooms might not display all four features, however. For example, the volva may not look cup-like. Instead, it may look like fringe at the base of the stem, but it is still a volva in structure.

The annulus is present when the mushroom is fresh, but it may shrink or fall off after the mushroom dries out. An Amanita such as this can appear to lack an annulus.

Therefore, you must not only account for the four features of Amanita mushrooms, but also these variables when examining a mushroom.

The genus *Amanita* is responsible for most mushroom poisoning deaths. It is very important to learn how to identify this group of fungi and avoid collecting any mushrooms with these characteristics. Many Amanitas are large, striking-looking mushrooms that grow in woodlands and are most abundant in the fall. It's ironic that these deadly mushrooms are not only favorite subjects of outdoors photographers, but they also are commonly used to illustrate children's books!

Fly agaric

Death cap

Destroying angel

Two common species of *Amanita* are the death cap (*Amanita phalloides*) and destroying angel (*Amanita virosa*). Consuming even a small amount of either of these mushrooms or visually identical species could be fatal. Avoid these at all costs!

The volva, or cup, of the Amanita is a structure that initially appears like a small Ping-Pong ball or golf ball and looks like a cup only when the mushroom matures. The cup, which in the early stages contained the entire immature Amanita mushroom, is called a universal veil. As the immature mushroom within the capsule starts to grow and expand, the cap pushes upward through the capsule, tearing through, or tearing off the top. What remains is the bottom of the capsule, which forms the shape of the cup.

Often the cup is covered by the soil and is overlooked by the novice mushroom hunter. It is very important to fully examine any mushroom to make a correct identification.

The annulus, or ring, is a membrane that attaches the edge of the cap to the stem and protects the developing gills. When the cap matures, it opens like an umbrella, separating the bottom edge of the cap from the annulus, leaving it attached like a skirt to the stem or to the edge of the cap.

White gills as a single characteristic are not a reliable indication of a poisonous mushroom, but when they are found in association with cups, rings and white spores, they spell trouble. Having white gills is not an indication of the spore color.

SPORE PRINT

Spore prints are easy to do on most mushrooms. Spore color remains constant and is unique to groups of mushrooms. This can be very helpful when identifying unknown mushrooms.

White spores are the rule for the Amanita mushrooms. To make a spore print, simply place the cap of the mushroom, gill-side or pore-side down, on a piece of white or black paper and cover the cap with a bowl or glass. (To help detect sparse spore prints, you may use clear, stiff plastic or glass instead of paper.) Let this stand for 30 minutes to 3 hours, and then examine the paper.

Under the bowl or cup, air currents are eliminated and the spores that are cast off are deposited directly on the paper. When enough of these spores accumulate on the paper, they become visible.

Amanita spore print

Poisonous Mushroom Myths

Most mushroom poisonings happen to mushroom hunters who rely on myths and don't try to systematically learn about mushrooms. These myths are just **not true**, and should never be taken seriously:

- You can cook the poison out of the mushroom if you cook it long enough.

- If you peel the cap of a mushroom, the poisonous part is removed.

- Cooking poisonous mushrooms with a silver spoon will turn the spoon black.

Mushroom Poisoning: What to Do

If you suspect mushroom poisoning, call your local poison control center and seek medical attention at once!

Allergic Reactions and Other Cautions

Some people can have allergic (histamine) reactions to wild or domestic mushrooms. An allergic reaction occurs when your body reacts to an ordinarily harmless substance, such as seafood or strawberries. About 15 percent of all Americans, and about 100 million people worldwide, are allergic to some substances. Others may experience reactions to wild or domestic mushrooms, like an upset stomach. These incidences are of unknown origin and are not allergic reactions to food, but they can be just as serious.

An allergic reaction to a mushroom is not a true mushroom poisoning, but it can still have serious side effects. Symptoms include runny nose, itchy eyes, rash and swelling of the tongue, or a full-blown systemic reaction that causes low blood pressure and unconsciousness. If you have food allergies, it is prudent to consult a doctor before eating wild mushrooms.

The best way to avoid ingesting poisonous or harmful mushrooms is to follow this advice:

If you can't positively identify a mushroom as an edible mushroom, don't eat it! When in doubt, throw it out!

Leave unidentified mushrooms where they are until you learn more.

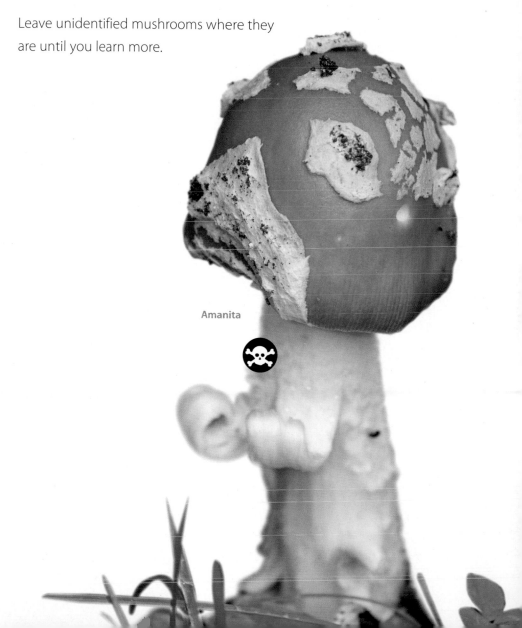

Amanita

How to Start Mushrooming

Raindrops fall from his wide-brimmed hat, landing on a carpet of golden leaves.

He has traveled this well-worn path for nearly a generation.

Autumn has been the time to escape to the woods in search for edible mushrooms, and this one is no different.

His only tools are a familiar walking stick and a tattered wicker basket.

Heavy is his basket but light is his heart upon returning home.

Hen-of-the-woods

IDENTIFYING THE SAFE SEVEN

For each of the seven *Start Mushrooming* species, you'll find text discussing each mushroom, photos, a checkoff guide and a seasonal quick-guide. The mushrooms are in order according to the seasons that they appear, beginning with spring. The seasonal icons under each chapter heading indicate the seasons in which the mushroom grows.

The text for each mushroom contains natural history, lore and harvesting tips. This section is meant to inform and also to inspire you to discover the real joy of mushrooming. Reading the text is essential to knowing the particulars of the mushroom.

Once you have searched for your mushroom in the appropriate season and habitat, and you've matched your specimen with the photos, you are ready to use the check-off guide. The check-off guide is designed to be a step-by-step process to help you identify your find.

The check-off guide is ordered from general to specific, so first check off the season, where the mushroom is growing and its overall shape. Then look for the specific characteristics of the cap, gills and stem.

Sulfur shelf

For each listed feature, observe, compare and decide if the characteristic is present or absent. Just as a tree either has leaves that are needle-like or flat and broad, mushrooms either have gills or they don't. A certain combination of characteristics adds up to a specific mushroom.

Be sure that all of the characteristics are present before you gather any specimens. If at any time you are not able to confidently check off all six characteristics, don't eat what you have found! Sometimes mushrooms take on unusual shapes. To be on the safe side, do not harvest mushrooms that don't match all of the characteristics and photos in this book.

Morel

USING THE CHECK-OFF GUIDE

The check-off guide for each mushroom always examines six characteristics. Here is a brief exercise using an abbreviated version of the guide. You'll see how easy it is to tell the differences among mushrooms by observing their characteristics one at a time.

Compare each photo to the three check-off descriptions. Examine the first mushroom and determine if the features are present or absent. Then do the same with the second and the third mushrooms.

☐ **OVERALL APPEARANCE:** Sponge-like appearance, ranging from tan to black in color.

☐ **CAP:** Cone-shaped or oval with many pits and ridges.

☐ **STEM:** Attaches directly to the cap.

You can see that only the middle mushroom (morel) has all three characteristics. Your identification correctly eliminated the left (oyster) and right (big red false morel) possibilities.

USING THE SEASONAL QUICK-GUIDE

The seasonal quick-guide serves to highlight key information about hunting for the mushroom featured in the chapter. It briefly describes when to look, where to look, how to find and how to collect. It is not meant to be a substitute for thorough reading.

For your first season or two as a beginning mushroomer, you'll want to comprehensively read all of the information and study the photos in this book more than once. In subsequent years and seasons, as you gain more experience, you may just want to review the information to refresh your memory, and then be on your way.

In any case, the more familiar you are with the features of a mushroom, the more focused you can be in your search.

Remember that to confirm your mushroom's correct identity, you must determine that all features described in the check-off guide are present.

To learn more about the types of information provided for the safe seven mushrooms in this book, check out the sample check-off guide and the seasonal quick-guide on pp. 36–37.

CHECK-OFF GUIDE

- **SEASON:** The growing season(s) of the mushroom, such as spring and summer.

- **HABITAT:** Sites where the mushroom grows, such as on the ground or on wood.

- **OVERALL APPEARANCE:** General description of the mushroom, including shape, size or color, with special features of the cap or stem. May include growth form, such as single or cluster.

- **CAP:** Specific features of the cap, such as shape, size, color or texture.

- **GILLS:** Overall description; may include color. If gills are absent, description of the pores (or wrinkles, as in chanterelles).

- **STEM:** Pertinent details of the stem, such as texture, color, size and attachment. If a stem is absent, description of the attachment.

Photos are shown with short descriptions

Oyster cap has a rolled edge

Long, thin gills

SEASONAL QUICK-GUIDE

WHEN TO LOOK: Spring, summer, autumn and/or winter.

WHERE TO LOOK: Type of habitat. More specifically, what the mushroom is growing on, such as the ground or wood.

HOW TO FIND: Tips about what to look for.

HOW TO COLLECT: How to hunt and gather without damaging the mushroom or the habitat. Tips about the parts of the mushroom that are best edible.

The Safe Seven

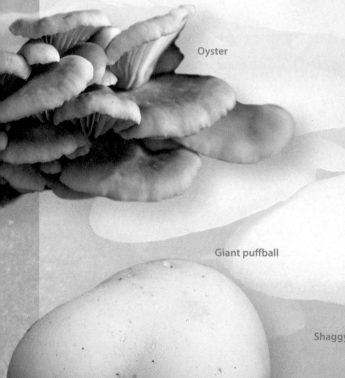

Oyster

Giant puffball

Shaggy mane

Hen-of-the-woods

Morel

Sulfur shelf

Chanterelle

Morel

MOREL

THE JEWEL OF THE MUSHROOM WORLD

Morchella spp.

Morchellaceae family

Spring   Summer

Some people view the morel as the crown jewel of the mushroom world. It is certainly the most sought-after mushroom in North America. Spring, and in high elevations, early summer, are the seasons for "morel madness"—a very contagious condition. It has been reported that ordinary people have turned into raving maniac morel hunters at the first sign of a new season!

There are as many as 20 species of morels in North America, and all are excellent edible mushrooms. Yellow, black and white morels are a few of the species, but all morels range from tan to black in color. Morels are sometimes called sponge mushrooms due to the honeycombed or spongy appearance of the cap. Morel connoisseurs will tell you that different species of morels not only look different, but they also taste different.

Morels depend on ample spring rains and warm temperatures. This is why south-facing slopes are the best hunting grounds (these warm up quickly during spring), and why a compass is a handy device for the morel hunter.

Morels also grow under the guard of prickly ash thorns. Going after these would be like giving blood at a blood bank, but without the cash payment. You may also find them in a patch of poison ivy. Morels do this on purpose! Be cautious!

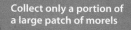

**Collect only a portion of
a large patch of morels**

Once the morels have come up, they will last several days to a week, depending on the temperature and humidity. The morel season itself lasts four to five weeks. If you are lucky enough to find a large patch of morels, it is wise to collect only a portion of the mushrooms. Leave the rest for others to harvest, and to allow the perpetuation of this coveted species.

Morel hunters use phenology to predict when morels will appear. Phenology is the study of the timing of natural occurrences throughout the year. Depending on the region, different signs indicate the beginning of the morel hunting season.

One of the more widely used signs in the eastern part of the country is when oak leaves become the size of a squirrel's ears. Some people use the blooming of lilacs, the sprouting of mayapple leaves or the flowering of trillium as their signal. Western morel hunters head for the hills the year after a forest fire. Getting in tune with your natural surroundings will help you to be a more successful morel hunter.

Morels occur throughout North America. A good place to begin searching for them is in forested areas and old apple orchards. In some western states, morels are known to grow under pine trees or in areas that had recent forest fires.

Morels are also likely to grow on or near floodplains of major rivers. Look for them in and around these low-lying areas.

Another good morel-finding spot is around dead elm trees. Here, the ground is often fertile for morels, but only for three to five years after the tree has died. The greatest crop grows the first year after the death of the tree, and production slowly declines after that. It is unclear why morels favor dead elms over other dead trees.

You can recognize a dead elm by its V-shaped silhouette and bleached trunk. If you are having trouble identifying a dead tree as an elm, compare it with other dead trees. Sometimes elms are associated with thick stands of prickly ash.

Look for morels around the circumference of any dead elm, out to 15–30 feet (4.5–9 m). Don't overlook small dead elms that have just started to shed bark. To find them more easily, fix the image of a morel in your mind by studying the photos provided. Then crouch down and scan the ground.

Huge flushes of morels occur after large forest fires. Search burned areas during the spring and summer after a fire.

Collect morels by cutting the stem with a knife or pinching it off at ground level. Always leave the underground portion undisturbed and healthy. Often, a new morel will sprout from the cut site.

Slice all morels in half vertically and inspect the hollow interior. Any mushroom with cottony material inside the stem or cap should be discarded.

Hollow interior

Cap has many pits and ridges, not folds or creases

Stem connects directly to the edge of the cap

The morel's stem should be directly connected to the edge of the cap. All morels have a cap with many pits and ridges, not folds or creases.

SPORE PRINT

The spore print of a morel is creamy yellow to white and varies widely. It is very difficult to obtain a print from a morel. The toxic *Gyromitra* species don't produce spore prints.

LOOK-ALIKES: FALSE MORELS

If you are not able to check off all of the morel characteristics in the check-off guide, chances are you have found a false morel (*Gyromitra* spp.). False morels are species of mushrooms that look similar to morels. However, false morel caps have many wavy folds and creases, not pits and ridges. The false morel stem (a vertical, rib-like white structure) is often solid or has varying amounts of cottony material inside it, rather than being hollow. As a false morel ages, sometimes the material in the stem shrinks, making the stem look hollow. No matter what is inside the stem, false morels are toxic and should not be eaten.

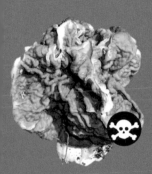

Gabled false morel

False morel

Big red false morel

GET OUT AND HUNT Remember, the time for collecting morels lasts only a few weeks each year. Note that the higher the elevation, the later the morel season starts. Don't let another season pass before you start mushrooming.

MOREL CHECK-OFF GUIDE

- ■ **SEASON:** Spring, and in high elevations, early summer.

- ■ **HABITAT:** On the ground. Around trees, grassy areas.

- ■ **OVERALL APPEARANCE:** Sponge-like appearance, ranging from tan to black in color. Most are 2–6 inches (5–15 cm) tall, though some can be much larger, ranging up to 12 inches (30 cm) tall.

- ■ **CAP:** Cone-shaped or oval with many pits and ridges. No folds or creases. Hollow inside, with no cottony material inside the cap.

- ■ **GILLS:** Absent. No pores.

- ■ **STEM:** Hollow, like a straw, with no cottony material inside the stem. Attaches directly to the cap.

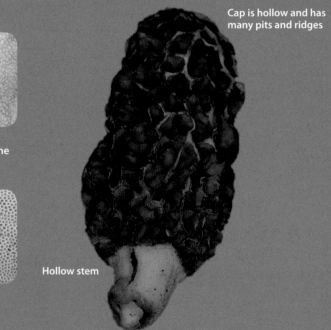

Cap is hollow and has many pits and ridges

No cotton-like material inside the cap or stem

No pores or gills

Hollow stem

SEASONAL QUICK-GUIDE

WHEN TO LOOK: Find morels during spring and summer.

WHERE TO LOOK: Look for them around dead elm trees, wooded sites, old apple orchards, burned areas and river floodplains throughout North America.

HOW TO FIND: Fix an image of a morel in your mind, and then crouch down and look across the ground.

HOW TO COLLECT: Cut or pinch off the stem without disturbing the underground portion. Slice in half to determine if the mushroom is hollow.

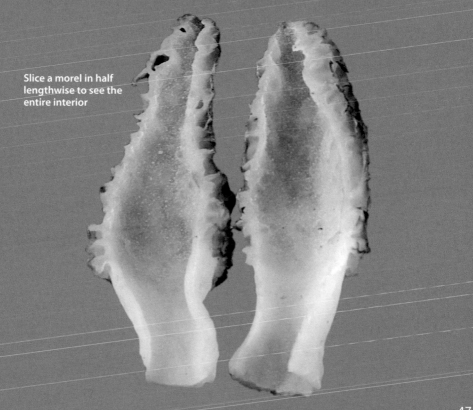

Slice a morel in half lengthwise to see the entire interior

Shaggy mane

SHAGGY MANE
THE EDIBLE URBAN MUSHROOM

Coprinus comatus

Coprinaceae family

Spring **Summer** **Autumn**

The shaggy mane gets its common name from shaggy-looking patches on its cap. It is also called the lawyer's wig because it resembles the old-fashioned wigs worn by lawyers during the Colonial Era. The cap and stem are white, and the cap is covered with small brown and white scales. Scales toward the top of the cap are typically darker reddish-brown and resemble a skullcap.

Fall is the best season for shaggy manes, but it is not uncommon to find them in spring and during a wet summer. Because they often grow in disturbed soils, they can usually be found along trails or playgrounds in your favorite park. They are also often found on newly established lawns where black soil was hauled in and deposited.

Shags are famous for mysteriously popping up overnight in suburban lawns. They have even been known to push their way through asphalt trails and tennis courts! This super-mycological strength is caused by a natural hydraulic process in which the mushroom transfers water into its cells as it expands. It seems that nothing can stop the shaggy mane from growing where it desires.

Shags like company, so look for them growing individually in groups of up to 100 mushrooms. They are usually 2–6 inches (5–15 cm) tall, but they can grow even higher.

When young, a shaggy mane looks like a small, cylindrical white mushroom cap growing on the ground with the stem hiding in the cap. As the stem grows and expands, it becomes exposed, while the elongated cap remains closed around the stem.

The cap is filled with white gills and can grow up to 6 inches (15 cm) tall. As the cap expands, the bottom edge tears away from the annulus, which is a ring that tends to be thin, flexible and slides freely up and down the stem, like a washer on a bolt. This is unlike the ring of an Amanita, which directly attaches to the stem. Because of the irregularity of the developing mushroom, a ring may not be found on every shag stem.

After the cap pulls away from the stem, the gills turn from white to a light shade of pink, to pinkish-red, and then reddish-brown as the cap begins the process of autodigestion. The shaggy mane belongs to a small genus with a handful of species found throughout North America. Known as the inky caps, they all share one common characteristic: the caps liquefy in a process of autodigestion, called deliquescence, in order to release their spores. Shaggy manes also release airborne spores before autodigestion.

Young shags

Shags break down into a black liquid containing millions of spores. The spore print of a shaggy mane is black.

This decomposition process is fascinating. The gills possess an enzyme that initiates the process of transforming the edible tissue into an inky mess. The cap first becomes black around the bottom edge. As the mushroom ages over the next several days, the process of autodigestion gradually moves up the cap until the entire cap is consumed. Only the cap is consumed; the stem remains intact.

When mature, observe that the stem is attached to the cap only at the top. This allows the cap to easily separate from the stem when the mushroom is fresh. Often you will see only the stems of shaggy manes with rings of black ink outlining each stem. The inky mess is easily rubbed on the fur of animals and on feathers of birds, or inadvertently eaten by animals as they graze on spore-laden grass. This transports the spores to new locations.

The base of the stem (at ground level) widens slightly, but it does not grow from a cup or volva, like that of an Amanita. To be on the safe side, examine the base for this feature during the first few times that you collect shaggy manes.

Shags liquifying
to release spores

Shaggy manes will begin to turn to ink soon after collecting, so it is important to cook or dry them right away. One way to store shags is to sauté them in butter and seal them in a container before freezing. I have been successful drying them, but only when they were gathered fresh, before the autodigestion process began.

Shags must be dried in a food dehydrator with a heat source that will dry them quickly at a high temperature. Air-drying won't work—they'll get inky before they can dry out. Other methods of storing, such as submerging them fresh in water or turning them upside down in an empty egg carton, do not increase the fresh life of shaggy manes. Fresh, frozen or dried, I find the taste of shags, both caps and stems, to be outstanding!

During cooking, the cap will shrivel to a fraction of its former size, so adjust your recipes if you are substituting other mushrooms with shags. They will also produce a great deal of liquid when cooking, which makes them superb for use in soups and sauces. I like to simply sauté them in butter with garlic.

LOOK-ALIKES: OTHER SPECIES

A close relative of the shaggy mane is the alcohol inky (*Coprinopsis atramentaria*). The alcohol inky differs from the shaggy mane in that it grows in tight clusters. Also, it is gray-brown, not white. Scales are rare on the alcohol inky; if they are present, they are only remnants and very small. Both species are edible.

Warning: The problem with confusing these mushrooms is that if you eat the alcohol inky and drink even a small amount of alcohol, you may get an upset stomach, along with vomiting and heart

Alcohol inky

palpitations. This is exactly why it is called the alcohol inky. Avoid drinking wine with dinner or having an after-dinner cocktail if you are eating this mushroom. Depending on how much of the alcohol inky that you eat, you'll need to abstain from alcohol for one to three days. With no alcohol, the alcohol inky produces no adverse effects.

The scaly inky cap (*Coprinopsis variegata*) is another confusing look-alike. This mushroom grows in clusters and is yellow instead of white. Also, the scaly inky cap grows on wood, such as fallen and rotting logs. This species has been known to cause adverse reactions in individuals and should be avoided.

The green-spored lepiota (*Chlorophyllum molybdites*) is a poisonous look-alike, but it is often much larger than the shaggy mane. It starts out with a round cap that flattens when it opens, unlike the shaggy, which has a cylindrical cap that never flattens. The stem of the lepiota often has a large and obvious ring. The spore print is green, as the name suggests. This mushroom can grow in your lawn, and it causes severe nausea and vomiting.

Scaly inky cap

GET OUT AND HUNT You don't have to travel very far to find the shaggy mane. You can often find it in your own yard.

Green-spored lepiota

SHAGGY MANE CHECK-OFF GUIDE

- ☐ **SEASON:** Spring, summer, fall.

- ☐ **HABITAT:** On the ground. Grassy areas, lawns, fields, along trails.

- ☐ **OVERALL APPEARANCE:** Single or in groups. Elongated oval shape, 2–6 inches (5–15 cm) tall, with a shaggy white cap.

- ☐ **CAP:** White with shaggy white-to-brown patches. Cylindrical shape with a rounded top, covering most of the stem, 3–6 inches (7.5–15 cm) tall.

- ☐ **GILLS:** White gills, tightly packed together. Gills turn pink, then pinkish-red to reddish-brown, and then black with age, bottom edge first.

- ☐ **STEM:** Single, fibrous and white, about ½-inch (1 cm) wide, slightly enlarged at the base. Attaches to the cap only at the very top.

Cylindrical shaggy cap

Fibrous single stem, slightly larger at the base

Shaggy mane has tightly packed gills

SEASONAL QUICK-GUIDE

WHEN TO LOOK: Find shaggy manes during spring, summer and fall.

WHERE TO LOOK: Look for them in open grassy areas, lawns and parks that are free of chemicals or fertilizers. Also search disturbed areas and along trails.

HOW TO FIND: On untreated green lawns, scan for obvious white mushrooms. In woods, look along grassy trails.

HOW TO COLLECT: Harvest a few shags at first and dig up the base to be sure that they don't have a cup (volva) under the surface of the soil. (See *Confronting the Enemy* on pp. 24–29.) If safe, collect the rest. Then try making a spore print. If it's green, discard the mushrooms.

Sulfur shelf

SULFUR SHELF
THE CHICKEN OF THE WOODS

Laetiporus sulphureus

Polyporaceae family

Spring   Summer   Autumn

If you have ever been out in the woods in the fall, you have probably already seen this mushroom. I can't tell you how many times friends were able to describe this mushroom in nearly perfect detail following a walk in the woods near a lake home or after a vacation. This mushroom does not resemble many other mushrooms, and it grows in such abundance that it will become your favorite edible mushroom.

The sulfur shelf grows on wood and is almost never found on the ground unless it's associated with buried wood. In rare cases, when a section of wood is buried, a sulfur shelf can appear to be growing on the ground. A sulfur such as this looks like an orange rosette.

It doesn't matter if a tree is alive or dead, standing or downed, or if it's just a log or a stump—the sulfur will grow on it. A sulfur shelf begins as several small, bright yellow, finger-shaped growths that quickly expand to a large, flat shelf, or bracket. Each shelf is semicircular and attaches directly to the wood without a stem.

The sulfur shelf takes its common name from its color and growth habit. The top side of the flattened shelf is strikingly bright orange or pink. The outermost edge, or margin, is rounded and sulfur-yellow, or pallid, which matches the underside color of the shelf.

The sulfur shelf is similar to the hen-of-the-woods in that instead of typical gills, they both have small pores beneath. However, the pores of the sulfur

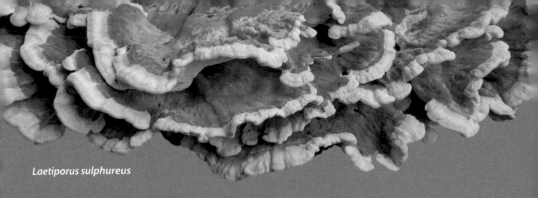

Laetiporus sulphureus

may be too small to be seen without magnification. As the sulfur ages, the color fades to dull orange and yellow. Just before it dies, the entire mushroom appears completely white, as though the color were bleached.

The sulfur may occur as a single shelf, but usually it grows in a large cluster of many overlapping shelves. This is a very impressive sight! A group of overlapping shelves can span 12–36 inches (61–91 cm) along a fallen log, making them a favorite subject for nature photographers. Each shelf varies in size from 2–3 inches (5–7.5 cm) up to 24 inches (61 cm) across. An entire young shelf can be harvested.

Large shelves yield tougher flesh and are less desirable as edibles. The outer edges of large, older shelves are the newest growths. Use a long, sharp knife to trim away this edible portion. Leave the portion of the fungi under the bark or wood undisturbed so that it may continue to grow.

SPORE PRINT

The sulfur shelf gives off copious amounts of spores. You can often see these on the surface of the mushroom. The spore print is white.

Depending on the amount of rainfall, the sulfur shelf fruits from spring to fall. It occurs throughout North America but seems to prefer different tree species throughout its range. It grows on live and dead deciduous trees, and is even known to grow on wooden decks! However, sulfurs growing on eucalyptus have been known to cause illness. Be on the safe side and don't eat these mushrooms.

Once you locate a sulfur shelf, be sure to check on it again in the future. A sulfur will often continue to grow in the same place as long as there are available nutrients in the tree or log and weather conditions cooperate. It can take many years to use all of these nutrients in a large oak or maple tree or log.

The sulfur shelf is also called the chicken of the woods (not to be confused with the hen-of-the-woods) due to its flavor. I think this is a misleading name because although the texture of the sulfur may be similar to chicken, to me it tastes nothing like chicken. The sulfur is considered to be a choice edible, meaning that it has exceptional flavor, and I couldn't agree more.

LOOK-ALIKES: OTHER SPECIES

In the past, the sulfur shelf (*Laetiporus sulphureus*) was considered a single species. However, recent investigation reveals there may be several species of sulfur shelf. These are now classified according to the tree species on which they grow.

In western parts of North America, from California to Alaska, the *Laetiporus coniferi-cola* grows on fir, spruce and hemlock trees. This sulfur shelf ranges from bright orange to salmon-orange and has a yellow surface below with pores. It is considered edible, but some people have reported gastrointestinal upset after ingestion.

Laetiporus conifericola

Laetiporus gilbertsonii

The identical-looking *Laetiporus gilbertsonii* is also found in western states, but it grows on eucalyptus trees. This sulfur shelf also has been known to cause gastrointestinal upset.

Laetiporus huroniensis

In the Great Lakes region, another look-alike sulfur shelf (*Laetiporus huroniensis*) grows on old-growth coniferous trees. This species is also edible, but once again, some people have reported upset stomach after consumption.

Perhaps the takeaway from these newly described variations of the sulfur shelf would be to not eat any sulfur shelf that is growing on a coniferous or eucalyptus tree.

The white-pored chicken of the woods (*Laetiporus cincinnatus*) is another closely related sulfur shelf. This mushroom is white with white pores and grows in a tight, round cluster, not overlapping shelves. It doesn't really look that similar to the safe sulfur shelf (*Laetiporus sulphureus*), but they can be confused.

White-pored chicken of the woods

The jack-o-lantern (*Omphalotus illudens*) is a poisonous mushroom that looks similar to the sulfur shelf in color, but it grows at the base of trees, often from a single stem, and has obvious gills, not yellow pores. Use the check-off system to eliminate this toxic mushroom.

As with all wild mushrooms, you should not eat a sulfur shelf raw. Collect the fresh, tender parts and cook them thoroughly. A hint to determine the age of a sulfur: your fingerprints from handling will show on the surface of a young sulfur, but not on an old sulfur.

GET OUT AND HUNT The sulfur shelf is a large and obvious mushroom that is easy to identify, making it easier for you to start mushrooming.

Jack-o-lantern

SULFUR SHELF CHECK-OFF GUIDE

- ■ **SEASON:** Spring, summer, fall.

- ■ **HABITAT:** On wood. Forests, backyards. To be safe, avoid sulfur shelves found on coniferous trees or eucalyptus.

- ■ **OVERALL APPEARANCE:** Large cluster of bright orange overlapping shelves, or brackets. Sulfur-yellow beneath. A cluster can range from a foot to several feet wide.

- ■ **CAP:** Fan-shaped or semicircular overlapping shelves.

- ■ **GILLS:** Absent. Many pores cover the entire surface beneath. Pores are sometimes too tiny to be seen without magnification.

- ■ **STEM:** Absent. Attaches directly to the trunk of a tree.

Sulphur shelf has many overlapping caps

SEASONAL QUICK-GUIDE

WHEN TO LOOK: Find sulfur shelf mushrooms in spring, summer and fall.

WHERE TO LOOK: Look for them in the woods on live or dead deciduous trees.

HOW TO FIND: From a distance, these are easy to spot due to the large size and bright orange and yellow colors.

HOW TO COLLECT: To harvest young, tender shelves, trim the soft outer edge of the older shelves with a knife.

OYSTER

THE SEAFOOD OF THE FOREST

Pleurotus ostreatus

Pleurotaceae family

Spring	Summer	Autumn	Winter

There are several oyster mushroom species, but they all look the same and all are edible. One of the identifying characteristics of oyster mushrooms is the lack of stems or stalks. Some may have a short or stubby stalk, but most are stalkless.

The common and species names of the oyster mushroom refer to the shape of the cap. The round clam, or oyster-shaped, cap has a rolled edge and can be pure white to buff-gray. When viewed from above, this mushroom is often described as a clam attached to a log by its hinge. Its pliable cap is smooth to the touch.

Finding oyster mushrooms is not difficult because they grow in great quantities. It is not uncommon to spot a large cluster from your vehicle while driving. However, the usual method to find oysters is to walk through the woods. A pair of binoculars is helpful to spot them on trees and logs in the distance.

Rainfall is the most important component of the oyster's life cycle, so get out and search for them within one or two days after a soaking rain. In dry years, concentrate your search along creeks and rivers because of the available moisture.

Oyster mushrooms fruit in early spring and throughout the summer, if the weather is favorable. However, they are more abundant in the fall.

The oyster is so eager to fruit that sometimes a large cluster will emerge in northern states on a warm winter day, only to be frozen that night. They may be harvested when frozen with a sturdy knife or small ax.

In the warmer southern states, the oyster fruits all winter with sufficient rainfall. Unless you plan to haul a ladder or bring a pruning saw with you on your hike, be prepared to tie your knife to the end of a long stick or climb a tree to get the mushrooms that are higher than your reach.

Begin searching in a deciduous forest known to have a number of downed trees—the favored growing medium for this delicacy. Oyster mushrooms grow in large overlapping clusters, or sometimes as a solitary mushroom, on dead aspen, elm, oak and maple trees, and, rarely, on conifers.

Oysters often grow on the same log year after year, so when you locate a site, return during favorable weather conditions to check for fruiting. Take a large collection basket because a typical patch can yield several pounds. In

Look for oysters growing on fallen logs or live trees

warm weather, the oyster decays quickly, so cook or dry your harvest as soon as possible. (See *Drying, Storing and Rehydrating Mushrooms* on pp. 114–121.)

The gills of the oyster mushroom are white and extend down to the attachment at the tree. An oyster's gills are so close together that you can fan them like the pages of a book. Note that this mushroom has white gills and a white spore print like the deadly Amanita, but don't worry—it lacks two other Amanita characteristics. The oyster does not grow from a cup, and it doesn't have a ring around a stem. In addition, it isn't terrestrial. Oysters grow only on intact, solid wood, not on the ground in soil.

SPORE PRINT

All oyster mushroom species are edible, and it's easy to obtain a spore print. The oyster print is white or pale lilac.

Harvest only soft and pliable oysters. As oysters age, they turn yellowish-brown and droop, becoming inedible. Check for small insects feeding on the oyster. Place your hand under an oyster cap and tap the top. A shiny black or red-and-black beetle may fall into your hand. This can mean that you found an oyster,

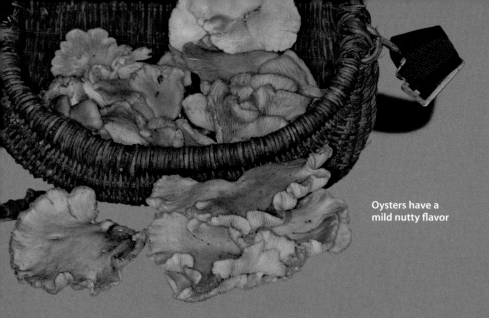

Oysters have a mild nutty flavor

but it also means that the beetles arrived first. These insects are easy to remove by hand or by submerging the caps in water. If the oyster is infested with white beetle larvae, the mushroom is not edible.

Some insects live and feed on specific mushrooms. Be sure to gather only the mushrooms you can use and leave the rest for the insects and other organisms. Insects play a major role in natural food chains and need these places to complete their life cycles.

Despite its name, the oyster mushroom doesn't taste anything like seafood. In fact, you'll find that they sometimes have a faint aroma of anise, especially when collected from aspen trees. Generally, this fleshy mushroom has a mild nutty flavor. You may find it on your grocer's shelves and served in restaurants since they are easy to grow commercially.

Oysters can be grown at home from kits or in large-scale production using wheat straw, sawdust, coffee grounds or egg cartons as a growing medium. It's not as easy as throwing some mushroom spawn (mycelium) on a pile of tea bags, but many people have been very successful at cultivating them. European cultivation of oyster mushrooms began in Germany after World War I, and now they are produced all over the world, including in the United States.

Oyster mushrooms are one of my favorites. They are easy to recognize, great to cook with and very common throughout North America. They dry well for long-term storage and can be available all year long.

GET OUT AND HUNT Oyster are a perfect choice for beginners. Purchase them from a local supermarket and examine them for the characteristics discussed. Then go out and start mushrooming for your own wild oyster mushrooms.

You can grow oyster mushrooms at home from a kit

OYSTER CHECK-OFF GUIDE

- ☐ **SEASON:** Spring, summer, fall, winter.

- ☐ **HABITAT:** On wood.

- ☐ **OVERALL APPEARANCE:** Large clusters of cream-colored, oyster-shaped, overlapping caps attached to wood. Some may have a short stalk. Can have the scent of anise.

- ☐ **CAP:** Semicircular, fan- or clam-shaped white cap with a rolled edge, 2–6 inches (5–15 cm) across. Can be depressed at the center or have a thin, wavy edge.

- ☐ **GILLS:** Long, thin and white, extending down to the wood. Some may extend down to a short stalk.

- ☐ **STEM:** Absent or may have a short or stubby stalk. Cap narrows to a stem-like appearance.

Oyster cap has a rolled edge

Long, thin gills

SEASONAL QUICK-GUIDE

WHEN TO LOOK: Find oysters year-round, especially during fall.

WHERE TO LOOK: Look for them in forests on the trunks of deciduous trees or on logs.

HOW TO FIND: While walking through woods, use binoculars to spot large clusters of white overlapping caps on trees in the distance.

HOW TO COLLECT: Cut oysters from trees without disturbing the mycelium underneath.

Giant puffball

GIANT PUFFBALL
THE GIANT OF FIELD AND FOREST

Calvatia gigantea

Agaricaceae family

Summer **Autumn**

The giant puffball is probably the best known of all fungi, and it is the one that beginners will most likely recognize. Each time I speak with a "mushroom skeptic," I use the puffball as an example of a mushroom that nearly everyone knows. I get the same response every time: "I didn't know that puffballs are edible. I usually just kick them." I privately grimace from the thought of kicking this delicacy!

There are many puffball species, but the giant puffball is the easiest one to identify. It cannot be easily confused with any other mushroom, except when the specimen is very small.

Giant puffballs are always found on the ground in groups of two or three, or in scattered singles. Look for them throughout North America in pastures, meadows, orchards, woodlands, and even on top of your compost pile. It is common for golfers to find what look like large, swollen golf balls on the course throughout the puffball growing season. Because all mushrooms readily absorb the chemicals commonly used to treat golf courses and lawns, avoid collecting in these areas. In fact, in any area where chemicals are used to treat pests, or where large amounts of fertilizer are used, you should not collect and eat mushrooms.

When harvesting puffballs, be sure that they have the firmness, color and consistency of a marshmallow. Don't confuse golf ball-sized puffballs with the young, developing stage of Amanita mushrooms. (See *Confronting the*

Enemy on pp. 24–29.) If you collect puffballs that are only baseball-sized and larger, there is no danger of confusing them with an Amanita.

The joy of hunting puffballs lies in the possibility of finding one that could easily feed your whole neighborhood. The giant puffball is one of the largest mushrooms, with record weights of 45 pounds (20 kg) and diameters of 24 inches (61 cm).

Giant puffballs develop from a pinhead-sized body and can grow to the size of a basketball. As a puffball reaches maturity, the skin and internal flesh are transformed from the edible white consistency to an inedible pale yellow, and then to olive-green. Avoid puffballs that are becoming pale yellow because they may cause diarrhea. The green interior is actually the maturing spores of the puffball.

Avoid discolored puffballs

The spores of the giant puffball and other puffball mushrooms are produced internally, rather than externally on gills. Spores are released through the skin as it cracks and peels during the aging process.

SPORE PRINT

The spore print of a giant puffball is green to brown. This mushroom only releases spores well beyond harvesting time and must crack wide-open to release them. Be aware that if you try to obtain a spore print, the mushroom can release trillions of spores. These could cause the air inside your home to become unhealthy.

Few youngsters have passed up an opportunity to kick an aging puffball and marvel at the "smoke" that comes out. Because the chance of one spore successfully landing on a suitable spot of soil is very low, this mushroom stacks the cards of reproduction success in its favor by producing copious spores. The puff of smoke is actually a reproductive insurance policy. I'm not sure who took the time to count spores, but the average puffball is said to hold 7 trillion of them, with large puffballs reaching upwards of 20 trillion spores!

Collect a puffball by cutting it at the base, or breaking it free by rocking it back and forth. Slice it through the middle. If it is snow-white, firm and free from insect damage, it is suitable for immediate use in the kitchen. A small amount of insect damage can be trimmed away as you would do with garden vegetables. If it is yellow or soft, discard it.

In early times, puffball spores and spiderwebs were mixed together and used as a coagulant to stop bleeding. Dried giant puffballs have been used as surgical sponges and as tinder for starting fires.

A puffball should have the firmness, color and consistency of a marshmallow

Puffballs regularly grow to the size of a human head. Long ago in Europe they were said to be mistaken for skulls lying about in a field, hence their morbid French name, *tête de mort*, meaning "head of death."

Early European settlers in North America, familiar with European puffballs, used the same species of North American puffballs as a regular food source during colonization. Additionally, several early American Indian tribes ate them as a substitute for meat in soups, simmered over a campfire.

A modern way to prepare puffballs is to cut slices up to an inch thick from the middle of the mushroom and sauté them in butter as if they were large mushroom steaks, or cut them into bite-sized cubes and sauté. Try the recipe for *Puffballs, Pasta and Peppers* on pg. 107. If you love mushrooms, this is a must!

GET OUT AND HUNT The giant puffball is an easy-to-spot mushroom and will make you happy that you decided to start mushrooming.

Hunt for puffballs in areas that are free of chemicals or fertilizers

GIANT PUFFBALL CHECK-OFF GUIDE

- [ ] **SEASON:** Summer, fall.

- [ ] **HABITAT:** On the ground. Fields, forests.

- [ ] **OVERALL APPEARANCE:** Close groups of two or three puffballs, or scattered singles. Round or nearly so, sometimes as large as a basketball, 2–12 inches (5–30 cm) wide, buff-white.

- [ ] **CAP:** Large and round, with irregularly smooth, thin white skin.

- [ ] **GILLS:** Absent. Solid white interior, with no structure of any kind within.

- [ ] **STEM:** Absent. Grows directly on the ground. Might have a cord-like "root" underneath.

Puffball cap is round and has smooth skin

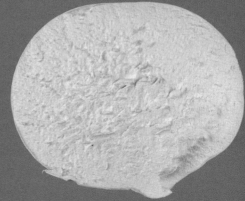

Solid interior with no gills

SEASONAL QUICK-GUIDE

WHEN TO LOOK: Find giant puffballs during summer and fall.

WHERE TO LOOK: Look for them in open fields, meadows, woodlands and orchards, avoiding any areas with chemical contamination.

HOW TO FIND: Search open fields for white objects that look like large, round rocks. Check again after heavy rains.

HOW TO COLLECT: Cut with a knife level to the ground, or rock the whole mushroom gently from side to side to break it free from the ground. Slice vertically and examine for: (1) insects; (2) solid white flesh; and (3) no stem, cap or similar structure. (See *Confronting the Enemy* on pp. 24–29.)

Chanterelle

CHANTERELLE
A POPULAR MUSHROOM WORLDWIDE

Cantharellus spp.

Cantharellus cibarius

Cantharellaceae family

Summer   Autumn

The chanterelle is a group of similar-looking fungi that are found worldwide. In addition to North America, they occur in Europe, Asia, Eurasia, Central America and Africa. They have many names, such as girolle, gallinacci or pfifferling, depending on where you live. Chanterelles are often light orange to yellow, funnel-shaped and meaty. As some of the most commonly sought wild mushrooms, they are truly an international delight!

The French first brought chanterelles into the culinary world back in the eighteenth century. The rich, firm body and delicate flavor made these mushrooms a favorite among discriminating chefs.

Today, Poland is the world's largest exporter of wild mushrooms, including the chanterelle. Many thousands of pounds of chanterelles, along with other mushroom species, are pickled and packed in jars and sold around the world. Sometimes you can find chanterelles in dishes at finer restaurants, when in season. One of the reasons they are so prized is for their eye appeal at the table. So far, they have resisted being cultivated and grown for production.

Chanterelles grow in multiples of up to several dozen, usually in mixed forests, and typically in shaded areas with a fair amount of moss or leaf litter. In some parts of the country, such as the upper Midwest, they are associated with conifers. In the western and eastern United States, they are associated with oak and beech trees. In other parts of the country, they can be found in birch forests.

Summer and fall are the best seasons for chanterelles. They are highly dependent on abundant rainfall. Once you find a chanterelle, stop and look around because there are usually many more. Chanterelles rarely fruit one at a time.

Chanterelles are usually pale orange or egg-yolk yellow. Less commonly, they are white. They have a distinct funnel shape, often with a wavy, rolled edge on the cap.

Underneath the cap are gill-like ridges that may feel waxy and run partially down the stem. These are considered false gills because they can't be cleanly separated from the cap or stem. The ridges fork (bifurcate), so look closely for them to divide. The stem tapers to the thinnest point at the surface of the ground.

Chanterelles are stout, full-bodied mushrooms, and they just feel good in your hands—not delicate at all. They have a very earthy aroma and smell delicious, often with a hint of apricot. The flavor is outstanding! Of course, they taste mainly like mushrooms, but they have a faint flavor of oak.

Some chanterelles stand 2–3 inches (5–7.5 cm) tall, with the very largest reaching 5–6 inches (13–15 cm). No matter the size, all are edible. They often grow in groups of over 20–30 mushrooms. Given the right conditions, you can gather many hundreds in one afternoon!

Chanterelles have a funnel-like, cup-shaped cap with a wavy edge

Chanterelles are fairly nutritious. They contain vitamin C and potassium, along with high levels of vitamin D. They hold up well during the cooking process, making them perfect and fun to use in recipes that call for lots of mushrooms. They are also excellent for pickling. They don't fall apart during pickling and pack well into jars.

SPORE PRINT

There isn't one specific spore print color for the chanterelles. Prints range from yellow to creamy white and light pink to dark salmon. Chanterelle spore prints are extremely difficult to obtain.

LOOK-ALIKES: FALSE CHANTERELLE

The false chanterelle (*Hygrophoropsis aurantiaca*) looks similar to *Cantharellus* spp. chanterelles, but it has true gills that are more brightly colored than the cap, and it forks much more. It is found in woodlands, often growing on woodchips. It is yellow to orange with a funnel-shaped cap, and it has a velvety texture. The stem is often not directly in the center of the cap. Also, the edge, or margin, of the cap is often rolled underneath.

Unlike the true chanterelle, the false chanterelle has narrow, forked gills running down the length of the stem. It often has an unpleasant or earthy smell, unlike the true chanterelle, which has a pleasant apricot scent. The false chanterelle is an edible mushroom but not a particularly good-tasting one. Some people have reported stomach upset after ingestion, so it is not advised to collect and eat it.

False chanterelle

Another similar mushroom that looks like a chanterelle is the jack-o-lantern (*Omphalotus illudens*), which is poisonous. The biggest difference is seen in the gills. The chanterelle has false gills, which appear like forked wrinkles. The jack-o-lantern has true gills—knife-like, paper-thin gills that don't fork. These gills will crumble and break away when you run your fingers roughly over them. The overall texture of a chanterelle is firm, not crumbly.

In addition, the jack-o-lantern grows in clumps or clusters, often from a single stem. The chanterelle grows individually. Jacks are usually much larger than chanterelles as well.

The jack-o-lantern grows around hardwood trunks, stumps and buried wood. The chanterelle grows in the dirt.

The jack-o-lantern is fairly bug resistant. Only a few beetles and slugs will reside in these mushrooms. Avoid the toxic jack-o-lantern.

GET OUT AND HUNT Now, let your knowledge guide you to a great chanterelle harvest when you start mushrooming.

Jack-o-lantern

CHANTERELLE CHECK-OFF GUIDE

- ■ **SEASON:** Summer, fall.

- ■ **HABITAT:** On the ground. Coniferous and deciduous forests.

- ■ **OVERALL APPEARANCE:** Single or small clusters, often in groups. Overall funnel-shaped, 2–6 inches (5–15 cm) tall.

- ■ **CAP:** Orange, yellow or white. Cup shape with a depression in the center and a wavy edge, 1–4 inches (2.5–10 cm) tall.

- ■ **GILLS:** False gills. Ridges, or wrinkles, run down the stem and typically fork, dividing the ridge into two. False gills can't be separated from the cap or stem without damaging the mushroom.

- ■ **STEM:** Single, fibrous and orange, yellow or white, about ½-inch (1 cm) wide, with a thinner base. Attaches directly to the cap with no joint, or to an area where the stem stops and the gills start.

Cap has a depressed center and a rolled, wavy edge

Ridges and wrinkles (false gills) run down the chanterelle stem

Single stem, thinner at the base

SEASONAL QUICK-GUIDE

WHEN TO LOOK: Find chanterelles during summer and fall.

WHERE TO LOOK: Look for them in coniferous woods and mixed forests, in moss or deep leaf litter.

HOW TO FIND: In undisturbed forests, search for obvious orange mushrooms growing in large numbers.

HOW TO COLLECT: Cut chanterelles with a sharp knife at the base near the soil.

Hen-of-the-woods

HEN-OF-THE-WOODS
A WOODLAND'S WONDER
Grifola frondosa
Meripilaceae family

Autumn

The hen-of-the-woods is considered one of the choicest edible mushrooms in the eastern United States and Canada, not only for its excellent taste, but also for its large size. That is why each fall many thousands of mushroom hunters take to the woods with a stout knife and a large basket. Hens grow as far west as the eastern slopes of the Rocky Mountains, but the usual range is the eastern United States and Canada, in deciduous forests. Depending on the region you live in, the hen-of-the-woods is sometimes called sheep's head.

Like an old reliable friend, the hen-of-the-woods can be counted on to fruit at the same location year after year. Most mushroom hunters have a favorite spot that they return to each year when autumn leaves start to fall. In fact, the Latin species name *frondosa* means "covered with leaves."

The hen grows on the roots of deciduous trees, especially oaks. The hyphae penetrate the roots of the host tree, causing what is known as white rot, and eventually damage the tree. This is an example of a parasitic relationship between a fungus and a tree.

The hen-of-the-woods can become very large, around 12–24 inches (30–61 cm) wide, making it easy to spot from a distance. A typical hen tops out at about 10 pounds (4.5 kg), but reports of up to an outrageous 100 pounds (45 kg) are not uncommon.

Hen-of-the-woods typically occurs alone, but lucky mushroom hunters sometimes find several growing at the base of an old oak tree. Each mushroom is made up of a tight cluster of many spoon-shaped caps and stems.

Upon close inspection, you will discover that the hen-of-the-woods grows from one central stalk and branches into many smaller stems. Each smaller stem has a lateral attachment, attaching to the side of each cap.

The caps are light gray to brown, and without too much imagination, they can appear to look like the feathers of a hen. Caps can be 1–3 inches (2.5–7.5 cm) wide. If you have ever seen a grouse hen and the varying sizes, shapes and colors of its feathers, then you have an idea of how a hen-of-the-woods looks.

The undersides of caps and stems are buff-white and turn yellow with age. Notice that there are no gills on the underside of the caps. Like the sulphur shelf, the hen has many small pores that function like gills to release spores. These pores resemble the surface of a sponge and extend partway down the stem (decurrent). The flesh is firm and brittle, white throughout and easily broken.

Hen-of-the-woods has pores, not gills

SPORE PRINT

A hen-of-the-woods spore print is white. The hen produces very large amounts of white spores, and prints are easy to obtain. Spores are often seen on parts of the mushroom directly below the pore surface.

LOOK-ALIKES: POLYPORES

A similar mushroom, the black-staining polypore (*Meripilus sumstinei*), is much larger than the hen-of-the-woods. It has gray caps, and white pores that bruise brownish to black when handled. Often appearing banded, it is tough and fibrous when pulled apart. Usually it is found associated with beech trees in the eastern United States.

Black-staining polypore

The Berkeley's polypore (*Bondarzewia berkeleyi*) is another similar-looking mushroom that also grows at the base of deciduous trees. However, the Berkeley's often grows to huge sizes, spanning more than several feet. The hen-of-the-woods does not. The Berkeley's has large overlapping caps, while the small caps of the hen are spoon-shaped. The pores on the underside of the Berkeley's are large and irregularly shaped compared with the hen's small, round pores. The Berkeley's is edible when very young, but it is bitter and inedible in later stages. More than likely you are not going to confuse these two species.

Berkeley's polypore

In Japan, the hen-of-the-woods is called the maitake (pronounced "my-TOCK-ee"), which means "dancing mushroom." The Japanese believe that the hen possesses a strong anti-tumor substance. They grow it commercially on sawdust for food and medicine.

Cooking with the hen-of-the-woods is a genuine pleasure! In addition to baking, frying and freezing, it lends itself to pickling. I highly recommend that you try the recipe for *Marinated Hen-of-the-woods* on pg. 111. A fresh hen-of-the-woods will last several days in your refrigerator, and it responds well to traditional drying methods. (See *Drying, Storing and Rehydrating Mushrooms* on pp. 114–121).

GET OUT AND HUNT A fresh hen gathered from the field smells as tantalizing as it tastes and is something to behold. Try the recipe for *Wilted Spinach Salad with Hen-of-the-woods Mushrooms* on pg. 110, and I'm sure you'll agree.

Find hen-of-the-woods at the base of deciduous trees

HEN-OF-THE-WOODS CHECK-OFF GUIDE

☐ **SEASON:** Fall.

☐ **HABITAT:** On the ground, at the base of deciduous trees (almost always oak).

☐ **OVERALL APPEARANCE:** Large and round, overall cauliflower shape, 12–24 inches (30–61 cm) wide. Multibranched, with many brown and gray overlapping caps that look like the ruffled feathers of a hen crouched on the ground.

☐ **CAP:** Numerous overlapping, spoon-shaped caps, 1–3 inches (2.5–7.5 cm) wide.

☐ **GILLS:** Absent. Many pores cover the entire surface under the caps and extend down the stems. Pores are round and are large enough to be seen without magnification.

☐ **STEM:** A central white stem branches into many smaller stems. Small stems attach to the sides of the caps.

Pores are under the caps and on stems

Caps overlap and are spoon-shaped

Central stem branches into many smaller stems

SEASONAL QUICK-GUIDE

WHEN TO LOOK: Find hen-of-the-woods during fall.

WHERE TO LOOK: Look for them in wooded areas, on the ground, at the base of live deciduous trees (mostly oaks) and dead stumps.

HOW TO FIND: Check around the base of live oak trees and dead stumps.

HOW TO COLLECT: Slide a large knife under the mushroom and cut the central stem at ground level.

Hen-of-the-woods fruit at the same location year after year

Cooking with Wild Mushrooms

When it comes time to eat, think mushrooms! It is often said that mushrooms are a superfood. Many ancient civilizations from around the world used mushrooms as a medicine. Today, they are touted as a functional food because they have potential positive effects on human health beyond the basic nutritional benefits. Some research shows mushrooms help with more than 200 human ailments.

There are many reasons to enjoy wild edible mushrooms besides their great flavors. Mushrooms have great nutritional value. They are a great source of fiber, a good source of protein and they provide important vitamins B and D, as well as potassium. They also are a good source of antioxidants.

The recipes on the following pages were selected to bring out the flavor and texture of each specific wild mushroom. Please remember to keep this in mind when substituting any safe seven mushrooms or store-bought varieties in the recipes.

For your convenience, most recipes include amounts for both fresh and dried mushrooms. For directions on rehydrating mushrooms, see pg. 119 of *Drying, Storing and Rehydrating Mushrooms*.

Chanterelle

Recipes: A Taste of the Wild

The butter twists and turns as it melts in the cast-iron pan. Strong earthy aromas rise from a basket of freshly gathered morels. The marriage is only moments away. With a dash of garlic, the ceremony begins. Coated in butter and seasoned to perfection, the morels are the honored guests. Enjoy!

Morel

Morel Mushrooms

Morel Honey-Mustard Chicken

INGREDIENTS:

2 cups fresh morel mushrooms or
   1 cup dried morels

2 tablespoons butter

2 chicken breasts, boneless and skinless

4 tablespoons Dijon-style mustard

2 tablespoons honey

dash celery salt

dash sweet basil

salt

black pepper

DIRECTIONS:

If using dried mushrooms, rehydrate them in warm water for 30 minutes or until soft (see pg. 119). Drain well.

Slice the mushrooms into strips and sauté in the butter. Wash the chicken. Whisk the mustard, honey and seasonings in a bowl. Coat both sides of the chicken with the honey-mustard sauce.

Bake in a preheated oven at 375° for 20 minutes or until the chicken is thoroughly cooked.

Smother in morel mushrooms.

Serves 2.

Stuffed Morel Caps

INGREDIENTS:

12 fresh morel mushrooms

6 tablespoons butter or margarine

2 tablespoons Parmesan cheese

garlic powder to taste

DIRECTIONS:

Use only fresh morels.

Cut the stems off the caps, and chop the stems finely. Melt the butter in a small saucepan. Add the chopped stems, Parmesan and garlic powder to the melted butter. Bring to a boil.

Spoon the mixture into the caps and arrange in a baking dish. Bake in a preheated oven at 375° for 10 minutes.

Serve hot.

Serves 2–4.

Morel Cream Cheese Spread

INGREDIENTS:

2 cups dried morels, chopped

3 tablespoons butter

¼ teaspoon garlic powder (not fresh garlic)

1 teaspoon parsley

3 8-oz. packages cream cheese at
    room temperature

DIRECTIONS:

Rehydrate the morels in warm water for 30 minutes or until soft (see pg. 119). Drain well. When rehydrated, morels look like coarse hamburger.

Sauté the morels in the butter. Stir in the garlic powder and parsley. Remove from heat and allow to cool. Then sauté until all of the water boils away, about 3 minutes. Beat the cream cheese until fluffy and fold in the morel mixture.

Refrigerate overnight.

Serve with crackers or crusty bread.

Dip option: If you prefer, whip in some milk to make a morel cream cheese dip.

Serves 12–16.

Shaggy Mane Mushrooms

Fresh Spinach and Mushroom Fettuccine

INGREDIENTS:

2 cups fresh shaggy mane mushrooms, sliced, or 1 cup dried shags

½ lb. fettuccine or linguini pasta noodles

2 cups fresh spinach leaves, washed and chopped

1 shallot (or onion), minced

¼ cup butter

White Sauce

2 tablespoons butter

2 tablespoons white flour

¼ teaspoon salt

1 cup chicken broth or veggie broth

black pepper

DIRECTIONS:

If using dried mushrooms, rehydrate them in warm water for 30 minutes or until soft (see pg. 119). Drain well.

Cook the pasta as directed on the package. Blanch the spinach in boiling water. Drain, rinse and set aside.

Sauté the shallot and mushrooms in ¼ cup butter. Set aside and keep warm.

White Sauce

Melt the 2 tablespoons butter in a saucepan. Stir in the flour and mix well. Add salt and the chicken broth. Simmer gently over medium heat until thickened; avoid boiling the mixture.

To serve, top the pasta with the spinach and mushrooms. Pour the white sauce over the entire dish. Dust with black pepper.

Serves 4.

Fresh Shaggy Manes and Vegetables

INGREDIENTS:

2 cups fresh shaggy mane mushrooms or 1 cup dried shags

½ cup cauliflower, chopped

½ cup broccoli, chopped

½ cup cabbage, chopped

½ cup carrots, chopped

4 tablespoons butter

½ cup water, if necessary

1 package instant chicken cup-a-soup

black pepper to taste

DIRECTIONS:

If using dried mushrooms, rehydrate them in warm water for 30 minutes or until soft (see pg. 119). Drain well.

In a large frying pan, sauté the mushrooms and vegetables in the butter. Add ½ cup water, if necessary. Add cup-a-soup mix. Stir well, but don't overcook; the vegetables should be crisp. Season with pepper.

Serve hot.

Serves 2–4.

Mushroom-Stuffed Tomatoes

INGREDIENTS:

1 cup fresh shaggy mane mushrooms or
   1 cup dried shags

1 small onion, finely chopped

½ clove garlic

1 tablespoon olive oil

1 teaspoon curry powder

dash salt and pepper

½ cup shredded mozzarella cheese

½ cup cottage cheese

4 large tomatoes, tops and centers removed

½ cup Parmesan cheese

DIRECTIONS:

If using dried mushrooms, rehydrate them in warm water for 30 minutes or until soft (see pg. 119). Drain well.

Sauté the onion and garlic in the olive oil. When the onion is soft, add the mushrooms, curry powder, salt and pepper. Cook over medium heat until the mushrooms soften, no longer than 5 minutes. Remove from heat.

In a large bowl, mix together the mozzarella and cottage cheese. Stir in the mushroom mixture.

In a baking dish, fill the tomatoes with the mushroom-cheese mixture and sprinkle with Parmesan cheese.

Cover and bake at 375° for 25 minutes. Uncover and broil until the top is browned.

Serves 4.

Mushroom Veggie Soup

INGREDIENTS:

2 cups fresh shaggy mane mushrooms, sliced, or 1 cup dried shags

2 medium potatoes, cubed

2 tablespoons butter

18-oz. can veggie soup broth

9 oz. can stewed tomatoes

2 cups fresh or frozen mixed vegetables

¼ teaspoon sweet basil

dash celery salt

black pepper to taste

Parmesan cheese

DIRECTIONS:

If using dried mushrooms, rehydrate them in warm water for 30 minutes or until soft (see pg. 119). Drain well.

Boil the cubed potatoes until tender. Drain and set aside.

In a large saucepan, sauté the mushrooms in the butter. Add the potatoes, veggie broth, stewed tomatoes and vegetables. Bring to a boil and add the seasonings. Cover and simmer for 20 minutes. Top off with Parmesan cheese.

Serve hot with bread and butter.

Serves 2–4.

Sulfur Shelf Mushrooms

Tasty Tomato and Sulfur Shelf Mushrooms with Macaroni

INGREDIENTS:

2 cups fresh sulfur shelf mushrooms or
   1 cup dried sulfur shelf mushrooms

2 tablespoons butter

2 cups elbow macaroni

1½ cups tomato juice, or soup

dash onion powder

dash garlic powder

salt and pepper to taste

DIRECTIONS:

If using dried mushrooms, rehydrate them in warm water for 30 minutes or until soft (see pg. 119). Drain well.

In a large saucepan, sauté the mushrooms in the butter. Parboil the macaroni (boil for only a few minutes) and drain.

Add the macaroni to the mushrooms. Pour in the tomato juice, or soup. Add the onion powder and garlic powder. Simmer until slightly reduced and the macaroni is cooked. Season with salt and pepper.

Serve hot.

Serves 2–4.

Shrimp and Mushroom Stir-Fry

INGREDIENTS:

2 cups fresh sulfur shelf mushrooms, chopped, or 1 cup dried sulfur shelf mushrooms

2 teaspoons cornstarch

2 teaspoons cold water

2 teaspoons soy sauce

dash Tabasco sauce

2 cups white or brown rice

4 tablespoons sesame oil

¼ lb. medium shrimp, peeled and deveined

1 small onion, sliced

1 green pepper, chopped

½ cup pineapple chunks

DIRECTIONS:

If using dried mushrooms, rehydrate them in warm water for 30 minutes or until soft (see pg. 119). Drain well.

Stir-Fry Sauce

In a small bowl, combine the cornstarch, water, soy sauce and Tabasco. Stir until the cornstarch dissolves.

Prepare the rice as directed on the package. Meanwhile, heat the oil to medium high. Toss in the shrimp and sliced onion. Stir-fry for 2–4 minutes. Add the green pepper, pineapple and mushrooms. Stir-fry for another 4 minutes. Add the stir-fry sauce and toss just to coat.

Serve on a bed of rice.

Serves 2–4.

Mushroom-Nut Pilaf

INGREDIENTS:

2 cups fresh sulfur shelf mushrooms or
  1 cup dried sulfur shelf mushrooms

1 clove garlic, crushed and chopped

5 scallions, chopped

¼ cup chopped walnuts

¼ cup chopped or slivered almonds

2 tablespoons olive oil

2 cups brown or wild rice

black pepper to taste

dash Tabasco sauce

DIRECTIONS:

If using dried mushrooms, rehydrate them in warm water for 30 minutes or until soft (see pg. 119). Drain well.

Sauté the mushrooms, garlic, scallions and nuts in the olive oil.

Prepare the rice as directed on the package. Toss the sautéed mixture and rice together. Season with black pepper and Tabasco sauce.

Serves 2–4.

Oyster Mushrooms

Mom's Old-Fashioned Potatoes and Oyster Mushrooms

INGREDIENTS:

2 cups fresh oyster mushrooms or
   1 cup dried oyster mushrooms

6 medium red potatoes, peeled and cubed

5 scallions, finely chopped

4 tablespoons butter, divided

DIRECTIONS:

If using dried mushrooms, rehydrate them in warm water for 30 minutes or until soft (see pg. 119). Drain well.

Boil the prepared potatoes until soft.

In a large saucepan, sauté the scallions and mushrooms in half of the butter. Drain the potatoes and add them to the mushroom mixture. With a fork or potato masher, mash the potatoes until smooth. Add the remaining butter in small amounts; extra butter may be added as needed.

Note: This potato-mushroom dish won't be smooth in texture, but that's the point of this old-fashioned recipe.

Serves 2–4.

Mushroom Fish Sauce

INGREDIENTS:

1 cup fresh oyster mushrooms, chopped, or
   ½ cup dried oyster mushrooms

2 tablespoons butter

⅓ cup chicken broth (or ½ bouillon cube)

¼ cup lemon juice

2 tablespoons shallots (or onion),
   finely chopped

1 small clove garlic

black pepper

4–8 tablespoons butter, softened

2 cooked fish fillets—your favorite kind

DIRECTIONS:

If using dried mushrooms, rehydrate them in warm water for 30 minutes or until soft (see pg. 119). Drain well.

In a medium-sized saucepan, sauté the mushrooms in 2 tablespoons butter. When the mushrooms are tender, add the chicken broth, lemon juice, shallots, garlic and black pepper. Simmer until liquid is reduced down to ⅓ cup. Remove from heat.

Drop the softened butter, one tablespoon at a time, into the sauce and whisk or whip until smooth.

Pour the sauce hot over steamed or broiled fish.

Serves 4.

Giant Puffball Mushrooms

Puffballs, Pasta and Peppers

INGREDIENTS:

2–3 cups fresh puffballs, cubed, or
   1 whole fresh, medium-sized puffball or
   1–2 cups dried puffballs

2 cloves garlic

½ cup peppers (green, red or semi-hot)

1 tablespoon olive oil

½ teaspoon basil

pinch tarragon

2 slices bacon, fat trimmed off, fried
   and crumbled

6 oz. evaporated skim milk

2 teaspoons cornstarch

dash Tabasco sauce, optional

6 oz. cooked pasta

DIRECTIONS:

If using dried mushrooms, rehydrate them in warm water for 30 minutes or until soft (see pg. 119). Drain well.

Sauté the garlic and peppers in the olive oil for about 2 minutes. Add the mushrooms and herbs. Sauté until the mushrooms are cooked, then add the bacon crumbles. Add 4 ounces of the evaporated skim milk. Cook and stir for about 2 minutes on medium heat.

Mix the cornstarch with the remaining 2 ounces of evaporated milk. Add the milk mixture to the mushroom mixture. Simmer and let thicken for about 2 minutes. Add Tabasco sauce if desired.

Serve over pasta.

Serves 2.

Onion-Garlic Mushroom Soup

INGREDIENTS:

2 cups fresh puffball mushrooms, cubed, or
   1 cup dried puffballs

1 large onion, chopped

3 large potatoes, chopped

1 clove garlic, chopped

2 tablespoons olive oil

4 cups chicken stock

2 cups fresh spinach leaves, washed

salt and pepper to taste

DIRECTIONS:

If using dried mushrooms, rehydrate them in warm water for 30 minutes or until soft (see pg. 119). Drain well.

In a large saucepan, sauté the mushrooms, onion, potatoes and garlic in the olive oil. When the onion and potatoes are soft, add the chicken stock and the spinach. Cover and boil the mixture for 15 minutes until the potatoes are well cooked. Allow to cool.

Pour the soup into a blender or food processor and puree. Return the soup to the saucepan. Bring to a simmer. Add salt and pepper to taste.

Serves 4.

Chanterelle Mushrooms

Chanterelle Soup

INGREDIENTS:

2 cups fresh chanterelle mushrooms, chopped

1–2 fresh chanterelle mushrooms, sliced lengthwise

2 shallots, minced

4 tablespoons unsalted butter

1 shot glass of brandy

3 egg yolks

½ cup cream

salt to taste

Soup Base

6 cups chicken stock

2 tablespoons butter

2 tablespoons flour

DIRECTIONS:

Use only fresh chanterelles.

In a large saucepan, bring the chicken stock to a simmer. In a small saucepan, melt the butter and stir in the flour until smooth. Add the mixture to the chicken stock. Simmer for 20 minutes, until ¼ of the stock has been reduced down.

In a large frying pan, sauté the shallots and chopped mushrooms in the butter, stirring often until the shallots are translucent. Add salt as desired. Add the brandy and cook until it's nearly gone. Transfer to a blender or food processor and puree. Add the puree to the soup base and simmer for 10 minutes.

Sear the sliced chanterelles in a frying pan until slightly brown. Set aside for the garnish.

In a medium bowl, beat together the egg yolks and cream. Slowly ladle a small amount of soup, a little at a time (so the eggs don't congeal), until a cup or two has been added. Pour the mixture back into the soup and simmer. Do not boil.

Garnish with the seared chanterelles and serve.

Serves 2–4.

Chanterelle Cream Sauce

INGREDIENTS:

½ lb. fresh chanterelle mushrooms, chopped

2 tablespoons shallots, finely minced

2 cloves garlic, finely minced

1 tablespoon butter

1 cup heavy cream

½ cup white wine

1 teaspoon chicken bouillon granules

½ teaspoon cracked black peppercorns

pinch of dried thyme

8 oz. sirloin or New York strip steak

salt and pepper

fresh parsley garnish

DIRECTIONS:

Use only fresh chanterelles.

In a large frying pan, sauté the shallots and garlic in butter until tender, or about 3 minutes. Add the next six ingredients and reduce heat to a simmer. Stir occasionally for 10 minutes. For a thicker sauce, add more heavy cream.

Rub the steaks with salt and pepper. Cook to desired tenderness on a grill or in a cast-iron pan.

Transfer to plates. Pour the sauce over the steaks and top with a parsley garnish.

Serves 2.

Hen-of-the-woods Mushrooms

Firehouse Chow Mein

INGREDIENTS:

2 cups fresh hen-of-the-woods mushrooms, chopped, or 1 cup dried hen-of-the woods

2 lb. pork butt, cubed

1 bunch celery, chopped

3 medium onions, chopped

¼ cup soy sauce

¼ cup blackstrap molasses, dark variety

¼ cup cornstarch

16-oz. can bean sprouts

chow mein noodles or long grain rice

DIRECTIONS:

In a large frying pan, brown the pork, and then move it to a large pot.

Add the celery, onions, soy sauce and molasses to the pot. Add enough water to cover and boil for 5 minutes. Let sit for 3–4 hours to marinate. Reheat and simmer for 30 minutes.

If using dried mushrooms, rehydrate them in warm water for 30 minutes or until soft (see pg. 119). Drain well.

Add the mushrooms to the pot and cook for 10 minutes. Mix the cornstarch with enough water to make a thick paste; stir into the pot and cook until thickened. Stir in the bean sprouts and heat until just warmed through.

Serve over chow mein noodles or long grain rice.

Serves 4.

Wilted Spinach Salad with Hen-of-the-woods Mushrooms

INGREDIENTS:

2 cups fresh hen-of-the-woods mushrooms or 1 cup dried hen-of-the-woods

5 oz. spinach leaves

2 tablespoons butter

2 tablespoons vegetable oil

2 tablespoons vinegar (rosemary, marjoram or thyme vinegars are recommended)

4 tablespoons honey

DIRECTIONS:

If using dried mushrooms, rehydrate them in warm water for 30 minutes or until soft (see pg. 119). Drain well.

Wash the spinach and arrange in salad bowls.

In a large frying pan, sauté the mushrooms in the butter. Combine the oil, vinegar and honey in a saucepan and heat to a simmer. Add to the mushrooms and mix.

Pour the hot ingredients over the spinach and cover the bowls. Let stand for 2 minutes.

Serve warm.

Serves 2–4.

Marinated Hen-of-the-woods

INGREDIENTS:

1 cup fresh hen-of-the-woods mushrooms, chopped

1 medium red onion, sliced into rings

10 drops hot pepper sauce or Tabasco sauce

½ cup vegetable oil

½ cup white vinegar

1 tablespoon sugar

1 tablespoon pimento, finely chopped

1 tablespoon parsley, finely chopped

4 cloves garlic, minced

DIRECTIONS:

Use only fresh hen-of-the-woods.

Boil the mushrooms for 5 minutes or until just becoming soft. Let cool.

In a large bowl, mix all of the remaining ingredients. Add the cooled mushrooms and mix.

Pour into a glass container and allow to marinate in the refrigerator overnight.

Serve cold as a salad ingredient.

Serves 2–4.

Recipe Notes

Drying, Storing and Rehydrating Mushrooms

Staring at the jars stuffed full of dried mushrooms, he was forever grateful to his parents and grandparents for teaching him the ways of the wild mushroom.

He will savor these mushrooms tonight with dinner and enjoy them forever in his memories.

Morel

MUSHROOMS ALL YEAR LONG

All mushrooms taste best when they are prepared soon after collection. But you may have collected more than you can eat in one meal. Preparing mushrooms for long-term storage is not difficult and takes very little time. During winter, there aren't many foods that compare to a plateful of freshly rehydrated hen-of-the woods or morels prepared for a dinner party with good friends. So not only can you enjoy your wild mushrooms fresh, but you can also value your dried mushrooms like gold throughout the year.

Dried morels

AIR-DRYING METHODS

I recommend air-drying your extra bounty. It is the method that best maintains the flavor and integrity of the mushroom. There are several methods of air-drying mushrooms. Choose the one that is the most convenient for your needs. I find that when it comes to drying large amounts of mushrooms, the simpler it is, the better I like it.

Drying time will vary with the amount of moisture in the mushroom, humidity in the air and the size of the mushroom being dried. Air drying works for all of the safe seven mushrooms except the shaggy mane. For instructions on how to dry shags, see pg. 52.

Before drying your mushrooms, wipe off any debris and trim off any dirt or rotten parts. Very rarely will it be necessary to clean mushrooms with running water. Washing will not injure mushrooms, but it might extend the drying time or require the addition of water to a recipe that previously didn't need it.

Like garden vegetables, a blemish on a mushroom may be trimmed and the remainder eaten. Avoid old mushrooms or any that are covered with unusual growth or color. Next, cut the mushrooms into manageable pieces and examine for insect damage.

When you want to dry just a few select mushrooms, simply place them on a well-ventilated windowsill out of direct sunlight. My favorite method for drying is to string the mushrooms with a stout needle on a strong thread, and then hang the string in a well-ventilated room or in front of an open window. A pleasant aroma fills the room and lasts for days as the mushrooms slowly shrink to half of their original size. Drying time is several days to a week.

The string method is very effective for all but the largest mushrooms. Simply cut larger mushrooms into smaller pieces and dry them on a string.

Strings of dried mushrooms have been used in expensive floral arrangements. You can use your dried mushroom strings in flower bouquets to decorate a den or kitchen until the mushrooms are needed for a meal.

String drying

For large amounts of mushrooms, using window screens is the most practical way to dry mushrooms. Simply lay the screens flat with blocks underneath to keep them off the ground and to allow air to circulate around all sides. Spread out the mushrooms so they don't touch each other and allow to dry.

The screens can be left outside in a shady area, away from squirrels and other animals that might think you have left them a treat. Drying time is three days to a week.

USING AN ELECTRIC FOOD DEHYDRATOR

Another way to dry mushrooms is with an electric food dehydrator. If the weather is too humid to air dry, or if space is a problem, a food dehydrator may be convenient. However, you'll want to consider two things: (1) it will generate heat in your home, so it may not be a good choice for summer; and (2) it consumes energy, while other more natural ways do not. If you do use an electric food dehydrator, set the temperature on the lowest setting for six to twelve hours.

TIPS FOR LONG-TERM STORAGE

You may wonder just how dry you want your mushrooms to be for long-term storage. If the moisture content is too high, mold will grow on the mushrooms during storage. If the mushrooms are too dry, they will be brittle and powdery. A happy medium is desired. The mushrooms should still be slightly flexible but not spongy when done. They should also retain a pleasant aroma.

HOW TO STORE DRIED MUSHROOMS

Storing dried mushrooms is as easy as putting them into a glass jar. Just about any jar with a tightly fitting cover will do. I find that an antique jar stuffed with dried mushrooms also makes a special gift or decoration. Be sure to label the jars with the name of the mushroom and the packing date.

Dried chanterelles

118

These mushrooms will last many years when dried and stored properly. Dried mushrooms on a string may be stored by hanging them in the kitchen next to the stove. Just break off the amount desired and rehydrate.

MAKE DRIED MUSHROOM SEASONING

Use some of your stored dried mushrooms to make a delicious seasoning. Mushroom powder is one of my favorite ways to season wild mushrooms and other foods. Using a mortar and pestle or a food processor, grind small, brittle pieces into a fine powder. Store the powder in a pepper shaker.

Use mushroom powder when cooking to flavor just about any main or side dish, including soups, stews and meats. You're going to love this variation on wild mushrooms! Think of mushroom powder as concentrated flavoring, and season foods to your taste.

Crush dried mushrooms into a delicious powder

REHYDRATING DRIED MUSHROOMS

All dried mushrooms are rehydrated in the same way. Place the mushrooms to be rehydrated in a medium-sized bowl. Add enough warm water to cover the mushrooms. Use warm, not hot, water. Let stand for up to 30 minutes. Small pieces will rehydrate faster than larger ones, so keep an eye on the process. You can test for proper moisture by squeezing. Each piece should be soft and pliable. Squeeze out excess water before cooking.

Try using chicken or vegetable broth instead of water for extra flavor when rehydrating. If you use water, save it and use as a substitute in any recipe that calls for chicken broth or vegetable broth.

Sulfur shelf

FREEZING: AN ALTERNATIVE TO DRYING

Freezing mushrooms is the next-best method to drying, but first the mushrooms must be cooked. Freezing mushrooms without cooking results in soggy mushrooms after thawing.

When a raw mushroom is frozen, the water within the cells of the mushroom crystallizes and ruptures the cell walls. Once the mushroom has thawed, the cell walls no longer can support or hold water. The consistency of uncooked, thawed mushrooms is soft and unpleasant.

To precook mushrooms, sauté them in a large frying pan using 2–3 tablespoons butter per 2 cups mushrooms. Allow the mushrooms to cool, and then pour them into a reusable, freezer-safe plastic container. Be sure to fill it to the top, eliminating as much air space as possible. Label and date it properly. The contents will be good for up to a year.

The World of Wild Mushrooms

Congratulations! You have taken the time to discover that learning to identify the safe seven mushrooms is not difficult. As an official mycophagist (someone who eats mushrooms—including the wild ones), you are ready to make each outdoor hike a new culinary adventure without the worry of making a deadly mistake.

I know you will enjoy discovering new places for hunting the safe seven mushrooms, as well as sharing the tasty recipes in this book with your friends. I hope that your appreciation of edible wild mushrooms will contribute to an environmental ethic in our country that includes good conservation practices.

If you want to learn even more about mushrooms, I encourage you to contact your local mycological society. The members can provide a wealth of mushroom knowledge, and you'll enjoy meeting people who share your passion for these edible delights.

Follow your heart and enjoy the world of *Start Mushrooming*!

Sulfur shelf

Bibliography

Edible Wild Mushrooms of North America: A Field-to-kitchen Guide. Fischer, David W. and Alan E. Bessette. Austin, TX: University of Texas Press, 1992.

Mushrooms Demystified. Arora, David. Berkeley, CA: Ten Speed Press, 1986.

Mushrooms of North America. Miller, Orson J. Jr. New York, NY: E. P. Dutton & Co., 1984.

Mushrooms of North America. Phillips, Roger. Boston, MA: Little, Brown and Co., 1991.

Mushrooms of the Northeast: A Simple Guide to Common Mushrooms. Marrone, Teresa and Walt Sturgeon. Cambridge, MN: Adventure Publications, 2016.

Mushrooms of the Northwest: A Simple Guide to Common Mushrooms. Marrone, Teresa and Drew Parker. Cambridge, MN: Adventure Publications, 2019.

Mushrooms of the Upper Midwest: A Simple Guide to Common Mushrooms. Marrone, Teresa and Kathy Yerich. Cambridge, MN: Adventure Publications, 2014.

National Audubon Society Field Guide to North American Mushrooms, The. Lincoff, Gary H. New York, NY: Alfred A. Knopf, 1981.

Observation Notes

Index

About the Author

Naturalist, wildlife photographer and writer Stan Tekiela is the author of the popular Wildlife and Nature Appreciation book series that includes *Wildflowers*, *Bird Nests* and the award-winning *Feathers*. Stan has authored more than 190 educational books, including field guides, quick guides, nature books, children's books, playing cards and more, presenting many species of animals and plants.

With a Bachelor of Science degree in Natural History from the University of Minnesota and as an active professional naturalist for more than 30 years, Stan studies and photographs wildlife throughout the United States and Canada. He has received various national and regional awards for his books and photographs. Also a well-known columnist and radio personality, his syndicated column appears in more than 25 newspapers, and his wildlife programs are broadcast on a number of Midwest radio stations. Stan can be followed on Facebook and Twitter. He can be contacted via www.naturesmart.com.